Lea Mahulla
Kl. BL212

Dirk Aßmann, Irene Hartwig-Hannemann, Thomas Meinen, Brigitte Nies

W0405452

Store and More

Alles auf Lager. Englisch
Fachlageristen – Fachkräfte für Lagerlogistik

2. Auflage

Bestellnummer 5087

Winklers
westermann

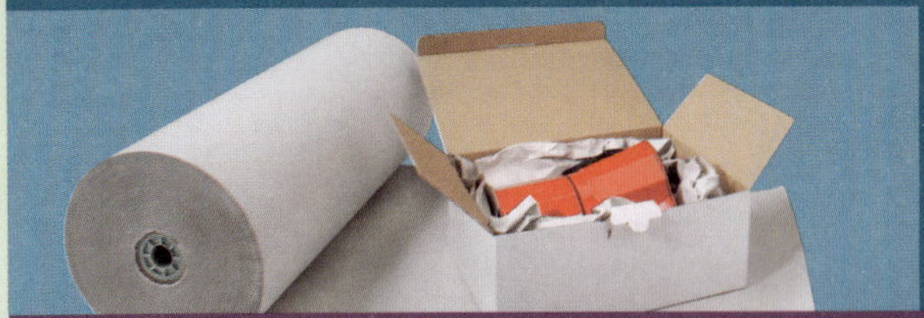

Querschnitt des Gebäudes

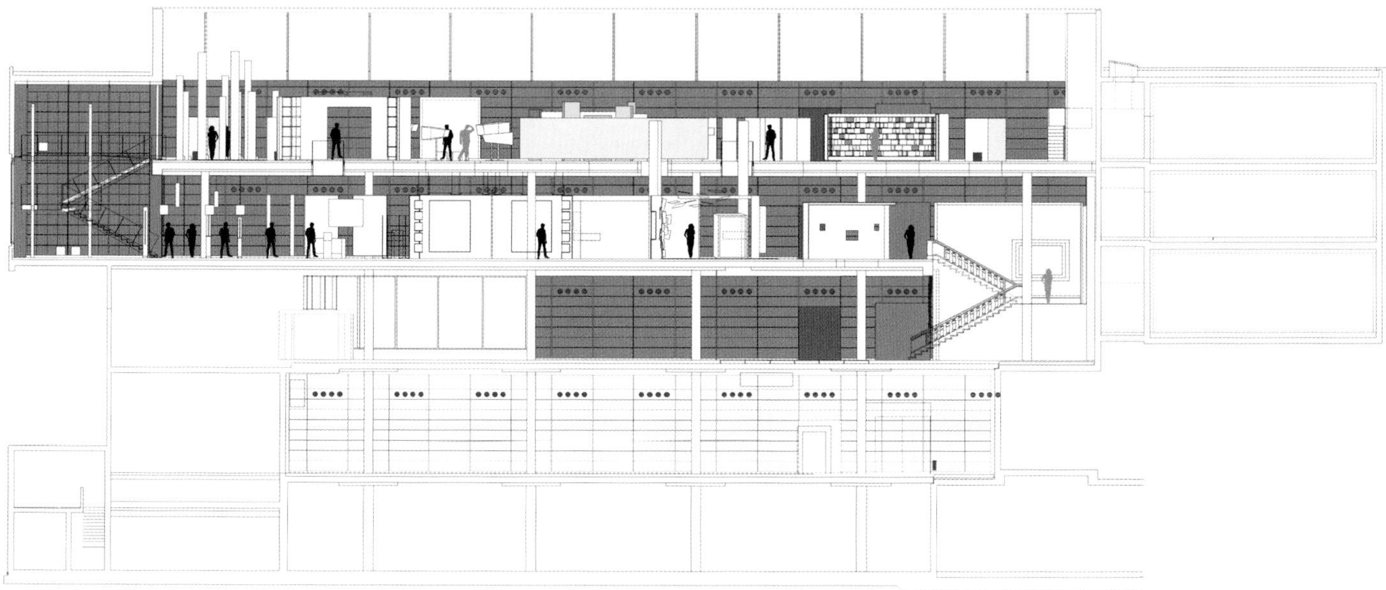

Abbildungen

Die Rechte an Fotografien und Filmen liegen, soweit nicht anders ausgewiesen, bei den in den Bildunterschriften genannten Personen und Institutionen. Alle weiteren Abbildungen ohne Nachweis: Haus der Geschichte Baden-Württemberg, Stuttgart. Fotograf: Bernd Eidenmüller, Stuttgart.

Albstadt-Tailfingen
Maschenmuseum 351

Amsterdam, Niederlande
Internationales Institut für Sozialgeschichte 119

Berlin
Digne M. Marcovicz 519
Helga Reidemeister 523

Bonn
VG Bildkunst 560, 561

Eppelheim
Alexandra Stock 95

Fellbach
Dietrich Sauter 180, 181

Freiburg
Augustinermuseum 336
Staatsarchiv 195
Stadtarchiv 89

Freudenstadt
Olfert Dorka 323

Friedrichshafen
Familie Spätling 487

Friedrichsruh
Bismarck-Museum 106

Goslar
Roberto Bona 106

Gundelfingen-Wildtal
Familie Nachbauer 494

Haslach
Hansjakob Archiv 428

Heidelberg
Sammlung Prinzhorn 168, 169
Klaus Staeck 262

Heidenheim
J.M. Voith AG 374

Karlsruhe
Güler Aydin 466
Badisches Landesmuseum 51
Generallandesarchiv 64, 117, 229, 355
Andrea Hoelscher und Norbert Nagel 474
Institut für Stadtgeschichte 419, 421
Landesamt für Umweltschutz 266
Staatliche Kunsthalle 54/55, 57, 334, 335

Kehl
Stadtarchiv 437, 441

Kellenried
Benediktinerinnenabtei St. Erentraud 461

Larchmont, New York, USA
Henry Froehlich 454

Lauterbach
Kunstverein Wilhelm Kimmich 336

Leutenbach
Tanja und Sandra Schnell 475

Lörrach
KBC 359
Museum am Burghof 223, 224, 225

Ludwigshafen
Ernst-Bloch-Zentrum 522

Marbach
Schiller-Nationalmuseum/ Deutsches Literaturarchiv 520

Ludwigsburg
Staatliche Schlösser und Gärten 88

Mainz
Stadtbibliothek 78

Mannheim
ABB 346
John Deere Archiv 362

Neuhausen
Günter Häussermann 182

New Ulm, Minnesota, USA
Richard P. Runck 444

Radolfzell
Guido Moriell 396

Saranac Lake, New York, USA
Lilo Levine 453

Schramberg
Junghans Uhren GmbH 358

Sigmaringen
Fürstlich Hohenzollernsche Hofkammer 51
Staatsarchiv 51, 66
Verwaltungsgericht 96

Speyer
Gerhard Kayser 128

Stuttgart
Jörg Amsel 296-301
Atelier Brückner 22, 23, 24, 25
Dr. Anneliese Braun 126, 129
Diakonie Württemberg 487
Hauptstaatsarchiv 65, 87, 144, 151, 162, 255
Max-Planck-Institut für Festkörperforschung 508, 509
Staatsanzeiger 261
Staatsgalerie 20/21
Familie Storm 475
Stuttgarter Zeitung 216
Wirtschaftsarchiv Baden-Württemberg 374
Württembergische Landesbibliothek 73, 78
Gerhard Ziller 505, 506

Triberg
Foto Carle 329
Werner Oppelt 310

Trochtelfingen
Ilse Hotz 456

Trossingen
Stadtbuch-Verlag Lienhard & Junge 217

Tübingen
Dr. Rolf Hein 343
Max-Planck-Institut für Entwicklungsbiologie 502
Stadtmuseum Tübingen 57

Tumlingen
Fischerwerke 345

Wannweil
Botho Walldorf 460

Weil
Dieter Korb 367

Wiesbaden
Bundeskriminalamt 268/269

Zürich, Schweiz
Schweizerisches Landesmuseum 92

Das Englischbuch „Store and More“ ist Teil der Reihe „Alles auf Lager“. In fünf Units werden wesentliche Themenschwerpunkte aus dem Berufsalltag von Fachlageristen und Fachkräften für Lagerlogistik behandelt.

„Store and More“ ist ein Lehr- und Arbeitsbuch, das den Schülerinnen und Schülern die Möglichkeit bietet, einen Großteil der Lösungen direkt in das Buch einzutragen. Diese Arbeitsweise erleichtert die Nachbereitung des Erlernten sowie die Vorbereitung auf Klassenarbeiten und Prüfungen. Die Inhalte des Buches orientieren sich am KMK-Rahmenlehrplan für die Ausbildung zur Fachlageristin/zum Fachlageristen und zur Fachkraft für Lagerlogistik sowie an den bundeslandbezogenen Lehrplänen für Englisch an berufsbildenden Schulen. Berufsbezogene Texte und praxisnahe Übungen dienen als handlungsorientiertes Training für alle wichtigen Lernebenen, Hör- und Leseverstehen sowie Sprachproduktion, Interaktion und Mediation. Das spezifische Fachvokabular wird in abwechslungsreichen Aufgabenstellungen eingeführt und geübt.

Jede Unit enthält wesentliche Bestandteile, die dem Buch eine klare und verständliche Struktur verleihen:

- Grammar boxes: Die Einheiten bestehen jeweils aus einer übersichtlichen Darstellung der wichtigsten Regeln der englischen Grammatik und darauf aufbauenden Übungen mit steigendem Schwierigkeitsgrad.
- Word banks: Zum Verständnis der Hör- und Lesetexte sowie zur Bearbeitung der Übungen ist schwieriges Vokabular in übersichtlich gestalteten Kästen aufgeführt.
- Tips and skills: Wertvolle Hinweise wie *How to start a presentation* oder *Appropriate style in business correspondence* dienen der Weiterentwicklung der Methodenkompetenz und erinnern an Besonderheiten der englischen Sprache.
- Business correspondence: Alle grundlegenden Formen der Geschäftskommunikation wie *Telephoning, E-Mails* und *Business letters* werden der Zielgruppe angemessen behandelt.

In einem umfangreichen Anhang können die Vokabeln nach Units gegliedert oder alphabetisch geordnet schnell nachgeschlagen werden. Die von Muttersprachlern gesprochenen Hörtexte sind auf einer dem Lehrerbuch, BN 5089, beigefügten CD enthalten. Der Schwierigkeitsgrad der Texte und Übungen ist gemäß dem Gemeinsamen Europäischen Referenzrahmen für Sprachen auf der Niveaustufe A2/B1 einzuordnen.

Autoren und Verlag wünschen viel Erfolg bei der Arbeit mit dem Buch. Anregungen und Hinweise sind jederzeit willkommen.

Winklers Verlag, Frühjahr 2017

Druck: westermann druck GmbH, Braunschweig

service@winklers.de
www.winklers.de

Bildungshaus Schulbuchverlage Westermann Schroedel Diesterweg Schöningh Winklers GmbH, Postfach 33 20, 38023 Braunschweig

ISBN 978-3-8045-**5087**-2

westermann GRUPPE

© Copyright 2017: Bildungshaus Schulbuchverlage Westermann Schroedel Diesterweg Schöningh Winklers GmbH, Braunschweig
Das Werk und seine Teile sind urheberrechtlich geschützt. Jede Nutzung in anderen als den gesetzlich zugelassenen Fällen bedarf der vorherigen schriftlichen Einwilligung des Verlages.
Hinweis zu § 52a UrhG: Weder das Werk noch seine Teile dürfen ohne eine solche Einwilligung eingescannt und in ein Netzwerk eingestellt werden. Dies gilt auch für Intranets von Schulen und sonstigen Bildungseinrichtungen.

1 My Business

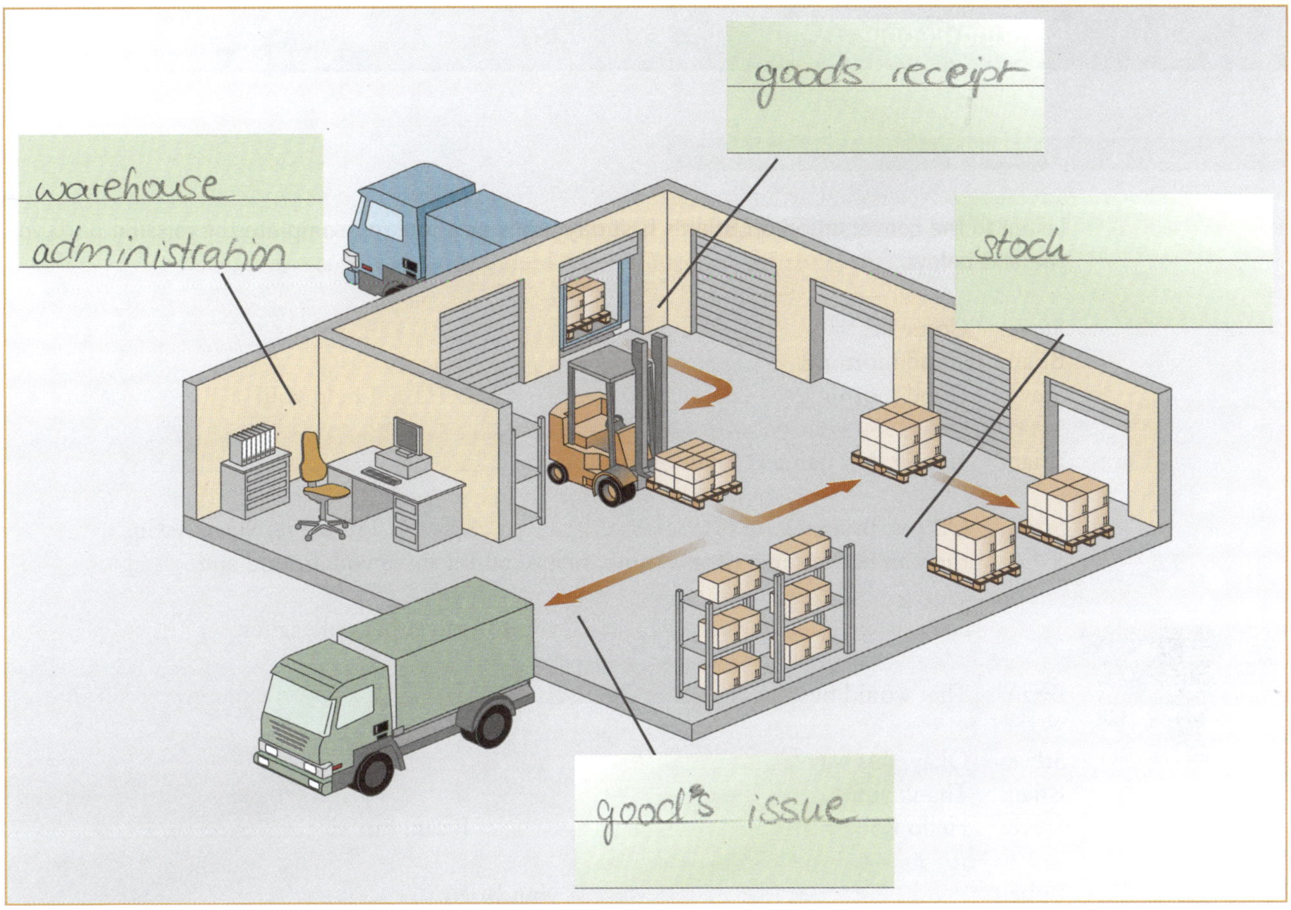

MATCHING

Look at the floor plan above and label the different warehouse areas with the correct terms from the box.

goods receipt | goods issue | stock | warehouse administration

DISCUSSION

a. Talk with a partner and make notes about his company and his workplace. Use the following prompts:
   - how did he/she find his/her apprenticeship
   - warehouse area he/she works in
   - company's name
   - location
   - number of employees
   - goods stored

b. Now present your findings about your partner to the class.

TIP
You can start your presentation like this:
– My partner's name is …
– He works in …
– He/she found the …

1

1.1. Meeting People

1.1.1. LISTENING

Listen to the conversation on Brian's first day in his new job and complete the missing parts in the text below.

Steve: Come in!
Brian: Good morning.
Steve: Good morning. ____________ I help you?

Brian: Yes, Sir. My name is Brian Stone, I'm the ____________ .

Steve: Oh yes, Brian, ____________ . I'm Steve, Steve Askins, the warehouse supervisor. I think, first of all I'll show you around and ____________ you to your other colleagues.

Brian: That would be ____________ .

Steve: Okay, this way ____________ .
Brian: Thank you.
Steve: Hello Robert, ____________ Brian, our ____________ .

Robert: ____________ you, Brian.

Brian: Hello, nice to ____________ .

Robert: We are quite busy today. A lot of goods ____________ and have to be stored and registered in the system. The guy over there ____________ is Allan. He is the one you will be working with.
Brian: I see.
Steve: I'll show Brian around ____________ . So he can get an idea of his new ____________ . I guess we'll be back within half an hour. Then you can introduce him ____________ .
Robert: Okay, see you later then.

WORD BANK

apprenticeship	Ausbildungsplatz
employee	Mitarbeiter
goods issue	Warenausgang
goods receipt	Wareneingang
location	Standort
stock	Lager
warehouse administration	Lagerverwaltung
warehouse operator	Fachlagerist
warehouse supervisor	Lagerleiter
workplace	Arbeitsplatz

1.1.2. MATCHING

Put the following dialogue between Sarah and David into the correct order.

- 1. Good morning. I'm Sarah Martin, the new apprentice.
- 3 Thanks, nice to meet you.
- 7 No, it's only ten miles away from Bristol.
- 9 Yes, I come by bus.
- 11 Oh, it's only a twenty-minute bus ride.
- 5 No, I'm not from Bristol. I am from Clutton.
- 12 So, it doesn't take too long?
- 4 Nice to meet you, too. Are you from Bristol?
- 8 How do you get to work? Do you come by bus?
- 6 I see, from Clutton. That's about 15 miles away from Bristol, isn't it?
- 2 Good morning, I'm David White. Please, call me David, we are not so formal around here.
- 10 And how long does it take to get here?

1.1.3. ROLE PLAY

Act out the following situation with a partner.

Ute Cremer holt Sandy Fisher am Empfang ab. Es ist der erste Tag in der Firma für Sandy Fisher.

Ute Cremer begrüßt Sandy Fisher und fragt, ob sie die neue Kollegin ist. →	Sandy Fisher bejaht die Frage und begrüßt Ute Cremer ebenfalls.
Sie stellt sich vor und heißt Sandy Fisher herzlich willkommen bei Futuristic Logistics Ltd. →	Sandy Fisher findet das nett und bedankt sich.
Sie möchte Sandy ihr Büro zeigen und bittet sie, ihr zu folgen. →	Sie bedankt sich.

HOW TO USE — The Verb "to be"

Positive Aussagen		Verneinung		Frage
I **am**	I**'m**	I **am not**	I**'m not**	**Am** I …?
you **are**	you**'re**	you **are not**	you**'re not**	**Are** you …?
he/she/it **is**	he**'s**, she**'s**, it**'s**	he/she/it **is not**	he**'s not**, she**'s not**, it**'s not**	**Is** he/she/it…?
we/you/they **are**	we**'re**, you**'re**, they**'re**	we/you/they **are not**	we**'re not**, you**'re not**, they**'re not**	**Are** we/you/they …?

1.1.4. EXERCISE

Fill in the correct form of the verb "to be".

Brian: Hi Sarah, (1) are you from London?

Sarah: No, I (2) am not from London, I'm from Liverpool. – And you Bob, where (3) are you from?

Brian: I'm from London – do you know London?

Sarah: Only a little but I know it (4) is nice there. Do you like the city?

Brian: Yes, I like London. It (5) is a great place. Many tourists visit the city every year, because there (6) are a lot of sights and a lot of things to do in the city.

Sarah: What (7) is your favourite place or sight of London?

Brian: Oh, that (8) is difficult to say. There (9) are a lot of interesting sights. For instance, there is the famous Buckingham Palace, the Tower of London and Big Ben. But there (10) are high entrance fees.

1.2. Inside the Company

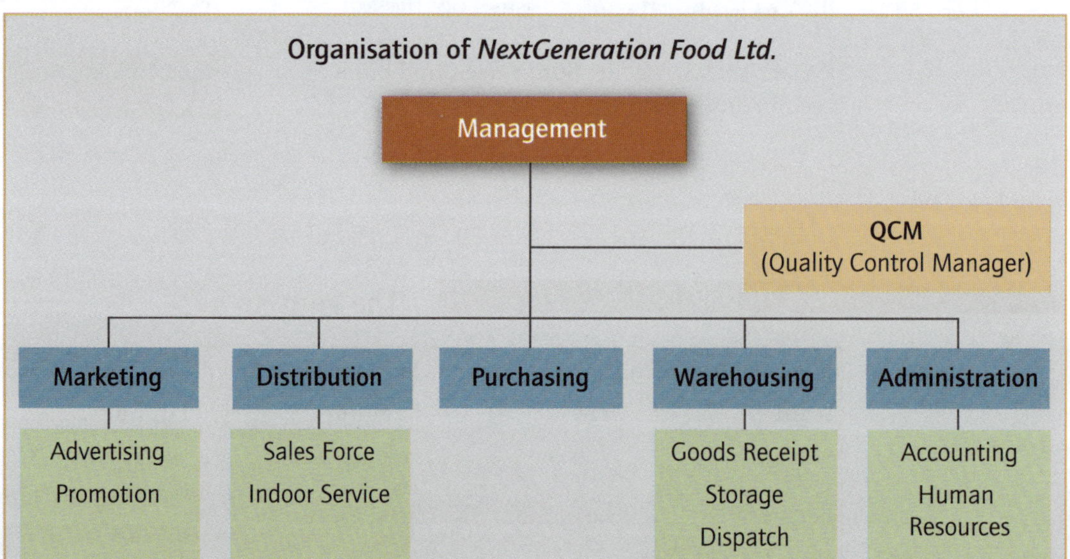

1.2.1. TRANSLATION

Find the German translations for the different departments of this company by using a dictionary.

1.2.2. ANALYSING

Refer to the organisational chart on page 8 and answer the following questions in complete sentences.

1. **If a customer wants to order something, which department does he/she contact?**

   They can contact the distribution

2. **Which department should interested candidates send their job application to?**

   They should send their job application to the administration

3. **Which department is in charge of placing orders?**

   The purchasing is in charge of orders.

4. **What is the responsibility of the marketing department?**

   They're responsible for advertisements

5. **By which department are the goods shipped to the customers?**

   The warehouse sends the goods

1.2.3. VOCABULARY WORK

Complete the company profile below with the words from the box.

~~business~~ | ~~distributes~~ | ~~farmers~~ | ~~needs~~ | ~~purchase~~ | ~~retail~~ | ~~success~~ | ~~team~~ | ~~warehouse~~ | ~~wholesaler~~

A Company Profile

NextGeneration Food Ltd. is a large (1) wholesaler of health food and organic food. The company (2) distributes a wide range of groceries to supermarkets, retail stores, restaurants and a large number of catering companies. It is a privately held company based in Tetbury. Operating all over the United Kingdom, a flexible distribution network helps to serve the customers' (3) needs.

We (4) purchase high quality goods direct from selected manufacturers and (5) farmers. Organic and naturally produced, healthy food is our mission as well as locally produced food. Our modern

(6) warehouse with high-tech storage equipment and processing technology makes us among the best in the food distribution sector. As part of our

(7) business concept, we provide customised service to our

(8) retail customers. We give our business partners great support and resources in terms of marketing techniques but also in logistics and technical issues.

The entire (9) team at *NextGeneration Food Ltd.* consists of experienced staff. These dedicated workers represent a key source of our

(10) success .

1.2.4. ANALYSING

Answer the following questions on the text above in complete sentences.

1. **What does *NextGeneration Food Ltd.* distribute?**

   It distributes health food and organic food.

2. **Who are the company's customers?**

   The customers are

3. **Where do the products come from?**

   They come direct from selected manufactures and farmers.

4. **What services does *NextGeneration Food Ltd.* provide to their customers?**

   They provide high-tech storage equipment and technology.

1.2.5. WRITING

Write a similar profile of the company you work for or a company you know.

WORD BANK

customised	kundenspezifisch
dedicated	engagiert
groceries	Lebensmittel
organic food	Biolebensmittel
to provide with	versorgen mit
to purchase	(ein)kaufen
staff	Belegschaft, Mitarbeiter
resource	Mittel
retail	Einzelhandel
success	Erfolg
support	Unterstützung
wholesaler	Großhändler

HOW TO USE

Present Simple

Anwendung:	
1. wenn etwas immer wieder passiert oder etwas immer so ist, Signalwörter: always, never, usually, sometimes, often etc.	I **work** for Futuristic Logistics.
2. wenn etwas im Fahrplan oder im Programm angegeben ist	He **watches** TV every night.
3. wenn man Gefühle, Gedanken, Meinungen ausdrückt	Robert **loves** his girlfriend.

Bildung:

Positive Aussage	**Verneinung**	**Frage**
I/you work	I/you don't work	Do I/you work?
he/she/it works	he/she/it doesn't work	Does he/she/it work?
we/you/they work	we/you/they don't work	Do we/you/they work?

Achtung:
- bei der 3. Person Singular (he/she/it) wird ein **„s"** an den Infinitiv des Verbs gehängt
- endet das Verb auf einen Zischlaut, wird **„es"** angehängt, z. B. miss – miss**es**, watch – watch**es**; endet es auf „y", wird dieses zum „i", wenn der Buchstabe davor kein Vokal ist, z. B. carry – carr**ies**

1.2.6. EXERCISE

Form negatives and questions out of the following sentences.

Example: The company distributes a wide range of groceries to supermarkets.
The company doesn't distribute a wide range of groceries to supermarkets.
Does the company distribute a wide range of groceries to supermarkets?

1. The company has its headquarters in Tetbury.

Has the company its headquarteis in Tetbury?
The company hasn't have its headquarters in Tetbury.

2. *NextGeneration Food Ltd.* operates all over the United Kingdom.

Does NextGeneration Food Ltd operate all over the UK?
NextGeneration Food Ltd doesn't operate all over the UK?

3. We purchase the goods direct from selected manufacturers.

Do we purchase the goods direct from the selected manufactures?
We don't purchase the goods direct from the selected manufactures?

4. **Our modern warehouse technology makes us among the best in the business.**

Does our modern warehouse technology make us among the best

Our modern warehouse technology doesn't make us among the best

5. **We provide customised service to our retail customers.**

Do we provide customised service to our retail customers?

We don't provide customised service to our retail customers.

1.2.7. LISTENING FOR GIST

a. Listen to three people talking about their jobs at *NextGeneration Food Ltd.* and complete the table below.

	Steven McPhery	Jennifer Humphry	Rosa Garcia
… works in which department?			
… has been with the company for how long?			
… finds his/ her job …			

b. Listen again and complete the following sentences.

1. I (1) ____________ the goods in stock.
2. Different types of goods (2) ____________ and handled in a different way, depending on their nature.
3. Keeping the (3) ____________ up to date is my job, too.
4. I (4) ____________ in this position
(5) ____________ last September and I like my work here at *NextGeneration Food Ltd.*
5. (6) ____________ and maintaining a good relationship with our

customers is the (7) ________________ of my job.

6. My job (8) ________________ is to increase the (9) ________________ of orders.
7. It is a very (10) ________________ and I don't know how long I will be able to do it.
8. I have been with *NextGeneration Food Ltd.* (11) ________________ .
9. Today, (12) ________________ two candidates for a vacancy in the purchasing department.
10. If we come to an agreement, we will sign an (13) ________________ .
11. Apart from hiring new staff, I also organise (14) ________________ .

TIP

Vocabulary
„es" in Verbindung mit einer Form von „to be" wird durch „there" wiedergegeben:
there is / there are: es gibt, es ist / es sind, es befindet sich / es befinden sich

there is / there's	There is no doubt that he is the boss.	Es besteht kein Zweifel, dass …
there are / there're	There are many mistakes in this business letter.	Es befinden sich …
Is there …?	Is there an elevator?	Gibt es …?
Are there …?	Are there enough goggles?	Gibt es …?

HOW TO USE Present Perfect

Anwendung:

1. wenn eine Handlung gerade stattgefunden hat oder ein Vorgang eine Beziehung zur Gegenwart hat, Signalwörter: just, already, ever, never, up to now, (not) yet	I **have** just **phoned** my colleague. I **have** never **been** to America.
2. wenn ein Vorgang in der Gegenwart noch andauert, Signalwörter: since (für Zeitpunkt in der Vergangenheit), for (für Zeitspanne)	I **have been** with the company for two years. I **have been** with the company since 2010.
3. wenn ein Vorgang in der Vergangenheit stattgefunden hat, aber der Zeitraum nicht genannt wird	He **has visited** London. I **have met** a famous person.
4. wenn der Zeitraum, über den gesprochen wird, noch andauert, Signalwörter: this week, today	The company **has grown** a lot this year.

Bildung:
Present Perfect = has/have + past participle (Verb + "-ed" oder 3. Form des Verbs)

Positive Aussage	Verneinung	Frage
I/you **have** arrived	I/you **haven't** arrived	**Have** I/you arrived?
he/she/it **has** arrived	he/she/it **hasn't** arrived	**Has** he/she/it arrived?
we/you/they **have** arrived	we/you/they **haven't** arrived	**Have** we/you/they arrived?

1.2.8. EXERCISE

Complete the following sentences by using the correct form of the verb in brackets.

1. We (1) have delivered (deliver) high-quality products to customers all over the world since 2010.
2. Our staff (2) have learned (learn) a lot in the computer course.
3. I (3) have never been (never be) to our subsidiary in Australia.
4. Look, Sarah (4) has bought (buy) a new car.
5. They (5) haven't yet dispatch (not yet dispatch) the ordered goods.

1.2.9. TRANSLATION

Translate the following sentences into English.

1. **Ich arbeite seit drei Monaten bei der Firma.**

I'm working in this company for three months

2. ***Next Generation Food Ltd.* ist Marktführer für Biolebensmittel geworden.**

Next Generation Food has become the market leader for organic food.

3. **Die Lieferung ist gerade angekommen.**

The delivery has arrived

4. **Die Verkäufe sind in den letzten zwei Jahren deutlich gestiegen.**

The sales ~~used~~ have increased since the last two years

5. **Tim hat die Waren bereits gepackt.**

Tim has already packed the goods

6. **Der Manager hat der Installation des neuen Systems zugestimmt.**

The manager agreed to the installation for the new system.

7. **Ich war noch niemals in Edinburgh.**

I've never been to Edinburgh.

8. **Wir haben uns in diesem Jahr ein neues Auto gekauft.**

We have bought a car this year.

1.3. Business Correspondence – Telephoning

1.3.1. READING

a. Adam McKinsey, the manager of the Edinburgh branch of *NextGeneration Food Ltd.*, has received the following e-mail. Complete the e-mail by using the prepositions from the box below.

by | for | in | of | to | with

From:	r.taylor@ngf.co.uk
To:	a.mckinsey@ngf-edinburgh.co.uk
Date:	10 October 20__
Subject:	Visit to Edinburgh branch

Dear Adam
As discussed earlier, the management is planning to install a new electronic order picking system (1) ~~for~~ in the Edinburgh warehouse. For this purpose I am arranging for a visit together (2) with our Director Ryan Montell and an engineer (3) of EasyStore at your site.
Would 9 August 20__ be convenient (4) for you to show us round.
We will come (5) by train to Waverly Station and would need a transfer (6) to the warehouse.
Please let me know if that will be okay with you.

Kind regards
Robin Taylor

From:	a.mckinsey@ngf-edinburgh.co.uk
To:	r.taylor@ngf.co.uk
Date:	10 October 20__
Subject:	Visit to Edinburgh branch

Dear Robin
I'm very sorry but we can't make it on 9 August as a number of staff including me are going to a full day training course. Would a week later be okay for you? I will be available any day except Tuesday.

Kind regards
Adam McKinsey

b. Adam McKinsey answered the e-mail on the same day. Read his reply on page 15 and answer the following questions.

1. Why does Adam McKinsey not agree to the visit on 9 August?

He's got a full training course on that day

2. What is his suggestion?

They could do that a week later

1.3.2. LISTENING FOR DETAIL

A day later, Adam receives a phone call from Robin Taylor. Listen to the conversation twice and try to fill in the missing words.

Robin: *NextGeneration Food Ltd.*, Robin Taylor speaking, how can I help you?
Adam: Hi Robin, this is Adam. Good to hear from you, how are you doing?
Robin: I'm fine, thanks, and you?

Adam: I'm fine, too – a little bit tied up with work, but (1) ______ smoothly.

Robin: I (2) ______ about Mr Montell's visit to Edinburgh concerning the installation of a new order picking system.
Adam: Yes, Robin. It's about arranging a date for the visit.
Robin: Right. The problem is that Mr Montell's schedule is very tight. This is why (3) ______ to arrange a date with you. You suggested the week after 9 August. Mr Montell (4) ______ with an important customer on Monday and the engineer is not available, too, he (5) ______ another company on Wednesday. So we've only got Thursday and Friday.
Adam: That's great for me. I'm only tied up on Tuesday.
Robin: So, let's fix it for Thursday then. Can you pick us up at Waverly at 10 o'clock?

Adam: Mmh, (6) ______ a briefing at 9:30 – but I think I can manage to be at Waverly at 10 o'clock.
Robin: Okay, fine. I'll arrange everything for our visit to your site.

Adam: Alright, (7) ______ forward to seeing you.
Robin: Me, too. See you then. Bye.
Adam: Bye.

HOW TO USE

Present Continuous

Anwendung:	
1. wenn etwas gerade im Augenblick des Sprechens passiert, Signalwörter: now, at the moment, right now etc.	I **am doing** my homework at the moment.
2. wenn etwas in der Zukunft fest geplant ist	He **is flying** to China next Monday.
3. wenn jemand etwas ausnahmsweise tut	Normally, I work in Hamburg, but today I **am working** in Munich.
4. wenn etwas zeitlich begrenzt ist	Brian **is working** at the company during the summer.

Bildung:

Positive Aussage	Verneinung	Frage
I **am** reading	I **am not** reading	**Am** I reading?
you **are** reading	you **are not** reading	**Are** you reading?
he/she/it **is** reading	he/she/it **is not** reading	**Is** he/she/it reading?
we/you/they **are** reading	we/you/they **are not** reading	**Are** we/you/they reading?

Achtung:
- endet der Infinitiv auf "e", so entfällt dieses, z. B. make – making
- nach einem kurzen Vokal wird ein Konsonant am Ende des Verbs verdoppelt, z. B. cut – cutting

1.3.3. EXERCISE

Present Simple or Present Continuous? Put in the verbs in the right forms.

1. Look! Betty (1) is going (go) to her car.
2. Ms Cohen (2) walks (walk) to work at 7:30 every morning.
3. The bus usually (3) stops (stop) in front of the station.
4. Mr Summer is busy, he (4) is writing (write) a letter.
5. The manager (5) is visiting (visit) the branch next Thursday.
6. The food in the canteen (6) tastes (taste) delicious.
7. Where are Charles and Bob? They (7) are loading (load) the lorry at the moment.
8. They usually (8) have (have) their lunch break from 12 o'clock to 1 o'clock.

1.3.4. READING

The Manager's Visit will be Soon

Mr Montell's visit is coming soon. The colleagues at the Edinburgh branch are busy arranging everything. Everything should **be in perfect order** when the manager comes to look around the warehouse. Even though he is only interested in installing a new electronic picking system the employees want to **make a good impression**. The warehouse staff are cleaning and clearing up their workplaces and the office staff are trying to **bring** their records **up to date**. They all are **looking forward** in eager anticipation to the boss's visit.

Adam McKinsey, the plant manager, is trying to book a hotel room for Mr Montell and his wife Susan Montell-Swenson as she has decided to **accompany** her husband at last minute. After their visit to the warehouse, they want to stay a little longer in Edinburgh and **do some sight-seeing**.

It is quite complicated to find a suitable hotel for the manager couple because it is high season and lots of tourists are in town. The annual event of the Military Tattoo also takes place at Edinburgh Castle in August. This event attracts a large number of visitors from all over the globe.

Find expressions in the text that have the meaning of the following German terms:

1. sich freuen auf	looking forward
2. in tadelloser Ordnung	be in perfect order
3. einen guten Eindruck machen	make a good impression
4. Besichtigungen machen	do some sight-seeing
5. etwas auf den neuesten/aktuellen Stand bringen	bring up to date
6. jemanden begleiten	accompany

1.3.5. WRITING

Make your own sentences using the expressions above.

WORD BANK

to arrange	ausmachen, arrangieren
to be tied up	beschäftigt sein
briefing	Einsatzbesprechung
demanding	fordernd
engineer	Techniker
to look forward to doing sth.	sich darauf freuen, etwas zu tun
to manage sth.	es schaffen, etwas zu tun
schedule	Zeitplan
smoothly	glatt, ohne Probleme
to suggest	vorschlagen
vacancy	offene Arbeitsstelle

1.3.6. LISTENING FOR GIST

Adam McKinsey has been on the phone all morning to find a hotel room for Mr and Mrs Montell. Listen to his phone call with the Calledonian Hotel and number the dialogue in the right order.

☐	Samanta:	You're welcome, Sir. Bye.
☐	Adam:	Good morning, this is Adam McKinsey of *NextGeneration Food Ltd.* I would like to book a double room.
☐	Samanta:	Certainly, Sir. When would you like to stay?
☐	Adam:	Oh, it's not for me, it's for our director and his wife. – They are arriving on Thursday, 18 August, and want to stay until Sunday, 20 August.
☐	Samanta:	Calledonian Hotel, Samanta Grey speaking. Can I help you?
☐	Adam:	No, Ms Grey that wouldn't help. We definitely need a double room. Thank you for your help anyway. I think I'll try the Hilton. Maybe they have a double room left.
☐	Samanta:	Just a second Mr McKinsey, let me check the system. – I'm awfully sorry, but there is no double room available for that time. Due to the Military Tattoo, we are fully booked. There are only three single rooms left.
☐	Adam:	Thank you, bye-bye.

1.3.7. ROLE PLAY

a. **With a partner, create a telephone conversation by using the activity cards. Write down the conversation.**
b. **Role play the dialogue.**

① Vincent Marony — ACTIVITY CARD

You receive a phone call from *Futuristic Logistics*. They want to hire a lorry. Take down the following details:

Customer name: ____________

Phone number: ____________

Date – from: ____________ to: ____________

Method of Payment: in advance ☐ Credit card ☐

Prices per day:		Lorry No 1	Lorry No 2
	one day:	£140	£115
	three and more days:	£115	£95
	features:	box, 7.5 tons, tail lift	curtain, 7.5 tons

② Peter Sommer — ACTIVITY CARD

Your work for *Futuristic Logistics*, Liverpool. Phone Number: 0721-789866.
Your lorry has broken down. Call *Express CarRental* in order to hire a lorry. You need it immediately for five days. It has to be equipped with a tail lift. You will pay by credit card when you pick it up tomorrow.

1.3.8. CROSSWORD PUZZLE

Find 12 hidden Past Participles in the grid and complete the table below. The first one has been done for you.

C	C	V	B	K	L	E	N	J	U	Z	Z
O	E	G	O	N	E	A	H	D	A	S	S
M	N	W	R	I	T	T	E	N	V	B	X
O	S	U	N	G	Z	E	L	G	B	M	Y
B	O	U	G	H	T	N	G	W	O	A	P
O	L	K	T	O	L	D	B	V	E	N	D
U	D	G	B	B	R	O	K	E	N	J	E
Q	V	N	G	F	I	N	T	Z	S	N	H
G	H	K	B	Z	B	E	C	O	M	E	X
N	O	T	T	F	R	I	G	Q	W	E	R

Infinitive	Past Simple	Past Participle	Deutsch (Infinitive)
go	went	gone	gehen
eat	ate	eaten	essen
write	wrote	written	schreiben
sing	sang	sung	singen
buy	bought	bought	kaufen
tell	told	told	erzählen
break	broke	broken	brechen
	became	become	werden

2 Warehouse Safety

DISCUSSION

The situations shown in the pictures above might look familiar to you. The daily work in the warehouse is full of surprises and dangerous situations. Describe the pictures above. Make up at least eight sentences. Feel free to use the words and phrases in the matching exercise.

MATCHING

Match the English words and phrases with their German equivalents.

d	1. workplace accident	a. einstürzen, zusammenfallen
a	2. to collapse	b. Lagerregal
e	3. forklift	c. Palette
f	4. to be injured	d. Arbeitsunfall
g	5. to load a lorry (BrE)/truck (AE)	e. Gabelstapler
b	6. storage rack	f. sich verletzen
c	7. pallet	g. einen LKW beladen

2

2.1. Dangers at Work

2.1.1. DISCUSSION

a. Work with your neighbour and tell him about critical situations you have experienced in your working life so far.
b. Discuss possible reasons why situations like these happen all the time and describe possible consequences for the employees and their employer.

Dangers in the warehouse	Critical situations	Reasons	Consequences
Employee	forklifts driving too fast, they almost run you over	employees are under stress / time pressure	employees, who are walking, could get hurt
Employer	employees don't wear proper safety requirements	they think, it's not necessary	employees could get hurt or even worse

2.1.2. ANALYSING

In order to analyse the cartoon, follow these steps:

a. List the objects or people you see in the cartoon.
b. Describe the action taking place in the cartoon.
c. Choose amongst the statements the one that expresses the message of the cartoon best. Explain your choice.

Statements:

1. Safety at work is just a waste of time.

2. No matter how busy you are, safety always comes first.

3. Safety at the warehouse is a purely voluntary aspect.

2.1.3. DEALING WITH DATA AND STATISTICS

Use the sources below to work out the most common causes for forklift accidents and useful strategies to prevent fatalities. Look at the boxes below.

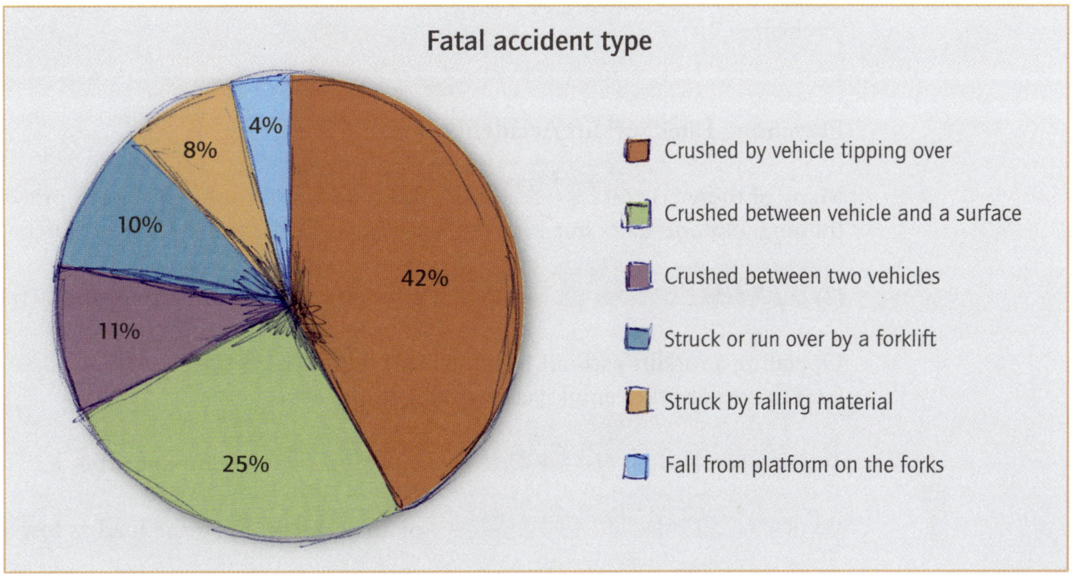

Chart 1: Fatal forklift accident causes

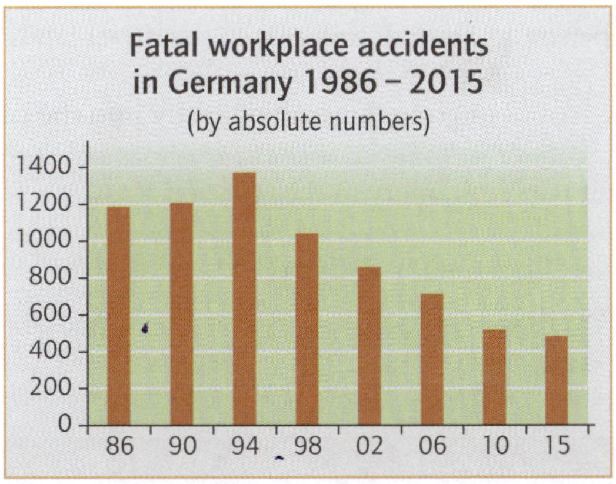

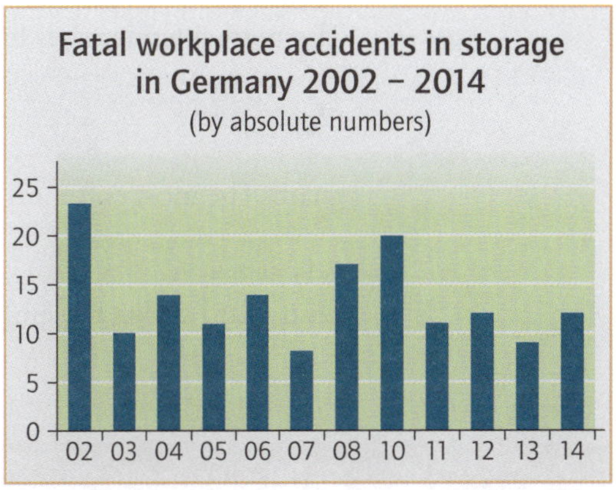

Charts 2 and 3: Fatal workplace accidents in business, industry and trade in Germany

SKILLS

Charts, graphs or statistics can show complex information in a simple way. Follow these three steps:

1. Describe – Name general information such as title and source of the graph etc. and the date of publication.
2. Analyse – Dealing with figures and numbers. Point out the most remarkable and important numbers. Leave out less important information.
3. Evaluate – Try to find answers to the main questions, e.g. "Why is the Chinese economy so strong?" State your opinion and feel free to speculate.

2.1.4. VOCABULARY

Read the following text and complete the gaps with the words in the box.

~~accidents~~ | ~~back~~ | ~~dangerous~~ | ~~drivers~~ | ~~floor~~ | ~~head~~ | ~~neck~~ | ~~operate~~ | ~~prevent~~ | ~~rule~~ | ~~severity~~ | ~~vehicle~~

Preventing Fatal Forklift Accidents

Many of these (1) accidents could have been prevented by better training. No one starts out with the knowledge, skills, and abilities to safely (2) operate a forklift. Drivers must be properly trained to do so.

Operating a forklift without training is (3) dangerous. It can even be fatal to you or other employees working in the area.

Training can also (4) prevent or reduce the (5) severity of an accident. Keep the load as low as possible to increase (6) vehicle stability and to help prevent tip-over accidents. Even if (7) drivers ignore this (8) rule and the vehicle tips over, injuries are usually minor if they stay with the vehicle instead of jumping off. The normal tendency is for a person to jump downward, so the driver lands on the (9) floor or ground, usually directly into the path of the overhead guard. The most common result is a crush injury to the (10) head, (11) back or (12) neck where the overhead guard strikes the employee.

2.2. Safety Issues

2.2.1. DISCUSSION

Read the statements below. Mark your position on the scales. With a partner, explain your choices. Then carry out a class survey and discuss the results in class.

	1	2	3	4	
Safety issues are of low relevance in my company.		X			Safety issues are of high relevance in my company.
I feel ill informed about safety at my workplace.		X			I feel well-informed about safety at my workplace.
Personally, I don't really care about safety at work.				X	Personally, I really care about safety at work.

2.2.2. LISTENING

a. Listen carefully to the report "Dangers in the Warehouse" and answer the following questions below.

What are the two major threats in a warehouse?

Which other health and safety hazards in a warehouse should you keep in mind?

b. Referring to health and safety hazards in a warehouse, which of these are the most relevant ones? Explain your choice. Point out possible avoidance strategies.

2.2.3. READING

Read the text you have just listened to. With a partner, discuss why the statements on page 26 are true or false.

Dangers in the Warehouse

Paul has been working at his company for six months. He has **become familiar with** the work in the warehouse. Right from the start he learned all the things warehouse operators normally do and his colleagues have been a big help to him. Paul has now got a better understanding of the complex processes in a warehouse and the **hazards** that might **occur**. At the beginning he was confronted with a huge number of laws and detailed instructions and regulations such as accident prevention regulations. His job includes a broad range of activities for example using and operating a forklift, loading and unloading and storing goods.

One of the most important things everyone in his company has to consider is how to avoid situations that might lead to **severe injuries** or even **fatalities**. There are basically two main **threats** to warehouse safety: in order to minimize fire hazards and to prevent accidents and injuries it is strictly **prohibited** to light a cigarette, to smoke or even to light a match. Flammable, explosive or chemical materials have to be stored in **fireproof** rooms. Fireproof doors should also be installed as well as fire exits and escape routes that lead to a safe place outside the building.

Last week, one of Paul's colleagues got fired because over the last two years he had stolen tools such as screwdrivers, pliers, electric drills, nails and screws. As a result of these thefts all workers at the warehouse had to take part in internal training with a special focus on 'Theft prevention in the warehouse'. The trainer explained that alarm systems, a clear storage system and regular checks would reduce the risk of theft significantly. Paul is surprised by the high attention his new employer pays to safety. His former manager did not care much about safety in the warehouse. More than once wrong behaviour and a lack of safety standards led to dangerous situations.

true (=T) or false (=F)

- [ ] 1. Paul does not get on very well with his colleagues because they ignore his problems.
- [ ] 2. Because of the risks, open fires are banned in a warehouse.
- [ ] 3. Laws and regulations of warehouse safety are for informational purposes only.
- [ ] 4. Paul's former employer had the same high safety standard as his current employer.
- [ ] 5. Fire exits and escape routes should be distinctively marked to avoid fatalities.

2.2.4. READING

After you have read the text carefully, answer the questions below the text in your own words. Do not copy whole passages from the text.

Warehouse Worker Injury Highlights Risk of Workplace Accidents

A worker at a textile **retailer** was injured after falling from a platform onto the **concrete floor** at the company's warehouse. The man had a broken leg and his **ankle** was **crushed** after a board had fallen onto it. He also received bad **bruising** to his face. The company had to pay **compensation** after it was found that workers had no supervision or training and no protection against falling from heights of up to 30 feet. They had not been given specialist equipment and the ladders that were used were unsuitable and not fixed.

Falls from a height are one of the main causes of workplace accidents across all industries but the warehouse holds other dangers, too. Another worker was hit by a forklift truck. The worker was **kneeling down**, measuring empty pallets when the truck ran over his right leg and hurt his foot. He broke three toes and fractured several bones in his foot. He had trouble walking for more than eighteen months after his accident.

Where vehicles and workers are in the same building there should be **measures** in place to ensure that both can move about separately and safely. Other hazards can include **slips and trips**, manual lifting and the collapse of storage systems. Storage areas should be carefully planned and regularly inspected. Pallets or shelves should be loaded in a way that ensures stability and should not be overloaded.

Every year, there are more than 10,000 workplace accidents in the storage and warehousing industries. Over 1,700 of these accidents are major injuries including fractures and amputation injuries. The number of accidents that occur is a clear indication that employers need to be taking more **precautions** to ensure the safety of their workers.

1. Which types of injuries are mentioned?

broken leg, crushed ankle, bruising, broken toes,

2. What are the reasons for the workplace accidents?

workers are not supervised and had no protection

3. How could the risks of workplace accidents be reduced?

there should be measures in places

2.2.5. MEDIATION

Your manager needs the basic statements of the article for an internal training. Unfortunately, he does not speak and understand English at all. He wants you to make a mediation of lines 7 to 16.

SKILLS

Mediation
To mediate a text means to sum up the main ideas and essential information the reader is looking for. Adapt your mediation to the reader's needs and feel free to leave out less important information. You do not have to translate the text.

2.2.6. INTERNET RESEARCH

Search the Internet for the keywords "forklift fatalities" to find more cases where forklifts were involved in serious accidents. Present your case to the class and explain what happened. Afterwards, start a discussion how to prevent such cases.

WORD BANK

ankle	Fußgelenk, Fußknöchel
to become familiar with sth.	mit etwas vertraut werden
bruise	Prellung, Bluterguss
compensation	Schmerzensgeld, Schadensersatz
concrete floor	Betonboden
to crush	quetschen, zerdrücken
fatality	Unglück, Todesfall
fireproof	feuerfest, feuerbeständig
hazard	Gefahr, Risiko
injury	Verwundung, Verletzung
to kneel down	sich hinknien, niederknien
measure	Maßnahme
to occur	auftreten
precautions	Vorsichtsmaßnahmen
to prohibit	verbieten
severe	ernst, schlimm, schwer
slips and trips	Rutschgefahr
theft	Diebstahl
threat	Drohung, Gefährdung

HOW TO USE Simple Past

Anwendung:	
wenn abgeschlossene Ereignisse oder Handlungen, die in der Vergangenheit stattgefunden haben, ausgedrückt werden sollen, Signalwörter: yesterday, last month, two days ago, in 2010, then, at that time etc.	We receiv**ed** the delivery **last week**. He clean**ed** the warehouse **yesterday**.

Bildung:
Simple Past = Verb + "**ed**" oder 2. Form des Verbs

Positive Aussage	Verneinung	Frage – Kurzantwort
I/you check**ed** it	I/you **didn't** check it	**Did** I/you check it? – Yes, you/I **did**. / No, you/I **didn't**.
he/she/it check**ed** it	he/she/it **didn't** check it	**Did** he/she/it check it? – Yes, he/she/it **did**. / No, he/she/it **didn't** it.
we/you/they check**ed** it	we/you/they **didn't** check it	**Did** we/you/they check it? – Yes, we/you/they **did**. / No, we/you/they **didn't** it.

Achtung:
- endet der Infinitiv auf "e", entfällt dieses, z. B. phone – phon**ed**;
- nach kurzem Vokal wird der Konsonant am Ende des Verbs verdoppelt, z. B. sto**p** – sto**pp**ed, pla**n** – pla**nn**ed;
- endet der Infinitiv auf "y", verwandelt sich dieses in ein "i", z. B. carry – carried

Ausnahme: Verb "to be"

Positive Aussage	Verneinung	Frage – Kurzantwort
I **was**	I **wasn't**	**Was** I? – Yes, you were. / No, you weren't.
you **were**	you **weren't**	**Were** you? – Yes, I was. / No, I wasn't.
he/she/it **was**	he/she/it **wasn't**	**Was** he/she/it? – Yes, he/she/it **was**. / No, he/she/it **wasn't**.
we/you/they **were**	we/you/they **weren't**	**Were** we/you/they? – Yes, we/you/they **were**. / No, we/you/they **weren't**.

2.2.7. EXERCISE

Put the verbs into the Simple Past.

Tom (1) founded (found) the company in 1999 and

(2) started (start) with six employees. They

(3) worked (work) very hard at the beginning and

(4) were (be) happy that the company

(5) ~~selle~~ sold (sell) their innovative products on the market.

The number of customers (6) rised (rise) constantly which

(7) led (lead) to a lack of capacity. Therefore, Tom

(8) decided (decide) to enlarge the company. In 2001, workers

(9) finished (finish) building the warehouse with approximately 2,000 square metres.

Soon, they (10) bought (buy) warehouse equipment such as

forklift trucks, pallet trucks and a shelving system. They even (11) purchased

(purchase) two lorries which (12) allowed (allow) them to deliver the goods directly to their customers and business partners. Looking back, Tom's decision

to invest in a warehouse (13) was (be) the right one and no one doubts that the warehouse has become one of the most efficient and well-structured departments.

Last year, the company (14) celebrated (celebrate) ten years of warehousing.

2.2.8. EXERCISE

Complete the sentences with one of these verbs. Put the verb into the correct form, positive or negative.

~~be | cost | enjoy | go | have | show | spend | stop | travel | visit~~

1. I was very tired, so I (1) went to bed early.
2. The book wasn't very expensive. It (2) didn't cost very much.
3. I (3) traveled by train with friends through Europe and we

   (4) visited a lot of interesting places.
4. Did you (5) show her the photos of your trip to China last year?
5. It was very hard work unloading the container. The boxes

   (6) were very heavy and bulky.
6. The PC game wasn't very exciting. I (7) stopped it very much.
7. Paul (8) spend a lot of money on clothes and PC equipment

   last month. Therefore, he (9) enjoyed making payments on his credit card.
8. I was in a hurry, so I (10) didn't have time to e-mail you.

2.3. Health and Safety Hazards

2.3.1. LISTENING

Listen to the report about safety in the warehouse. Which of the following hazards are mentioned? Underline the correct ones.

a lack of concentration | a nasty boss | broken glass | bad weather | drunk worker | lack of communication | long working hours | loud music | open fire | playing children | private problems | regular trainings | too heavy objects | wires or cables on the floor

Safety in the Warehouse

Working in a warehouse can be dangerous but it does not have to be. Besides workplace hazards, many injuries come from worker safety issues like **manual handling** injuries. Manual handling injuries are quite **common** especially among **novice** warehouse workers. These injuries can be caused by lifting heavy objects, long hours of carrying heavy loads, pulling items, pushing cargo items, and even holding such items. Sometimes a bad movement or just long hours at work can cause severe injuries. Before hiring employees, training should be given to new employees on lifting techniques, stretches and good **posture**. This training should be repeated every few months for all employees.

Other risks may come from hazards in the warehouse. These hazards include items lying around the platforms and workspace, not paying attention, lack of communication between employees and anything that seems out of place. There are ways to **avoid** such hazards. Some of these safety regulations may include daily **inspections** of the warehouse for possible hazards, speaking with the workers about potential safety hazards, or creating a team of employees to go over past cases of worker injuries and warehouse hazards in order to **pinpoint** which hazards and injuries are most common in your warehouse.

Sometimes there are many accidents in the workplace because of the layout design of the warehouse. Warehouses should have **ample** space to move about. Since workers are carrying heavy loads, the space should be open to avoid anyone **bumping** into anything. To decrease manual handling injuries the weight of objects carried should not **exceed** the weight that one can carry, push, pull, etc. Items should also be easy to carry. If items are hard to hold onto, **oddly** shaped or are easily droppable then there should be other options provided to carry these items in order to avoid injuries.

In order to eliminate the hazards in a warehouse and to increase warehouse safety, the **entire staff** needs to work as a team. If there are items lying around, like broken glass, wires or cables, these hazards should be reported to supervisors. Safety should always be every company‘s number one concern. If the workers are injured, no business will take place. But if the workers stay safe and obey worker‘s safety regulations in the warehouse then the company can make a profit.

2.3.2. READING

Read the text and put these paragraph summaries in the correct order.

- [ ] Teamwork is the key to successful occupational safety in a warehouse.
- [ ] In order to prevent manual handling injuries, special training should be given to the staff.
- [ ] The structure of the warehouse itself as well as the shape, weight and size of the goods are determining the risks.
- [ ] Laws, regulations and internal guidelines include a broad range of measures to avoid accidents and injuries.

2.3.3. VOCABULARY WORK

Find ten nouns from the text "Safety in the Warehouse" in the word field puzzle.

H	P	V	P	R	O	F	I	T	T	Y	W	V
Y	Q	Y	A	C	C	I	D	E	N	T	S	G
I	K	M	H	O	O	Y	I	A	J	Y	U	G
O	H	Z	X	C	L	N	C	N	T	U	J	I
G	D	Y	O	L	J	S	E	E	A	P	W	K
V	K	P	G	U	W	O	S	E	S	C	O	H
H	H	H	R	E	L	U	M	B	S	G	Z	T
F	O	I	I	U	O	K	P	L	Q	J	G	F
Q	E	G	F	H	G	N	I	N	I	A	R	T
S	H	I	E	E	M	P	L	O	Y	E	E	S
T	C	R	Y	N	A	P	M	O	C	X	Q	S
A	A	E	C	A	P	S	K	R	O	W	G	O
W	N	H	E	T	B	U	S	I	N	E	S	S

WORD BANK

ample	geräumig, ausgiebig
to avoid	verhindern
to bump into sth./so.	mit etwas/jemandem zusammenstoßen
common	alltäglich, häufig, bekannt
entire	ganz, komplett
to exceed	übertreffen
inspection	Prüfung, Kontrolle
manual handling	manuelle Handhabung
novice	Anfänger, Neuling
odd	seltsam
to pinpoint	genau bestimmen, festlegen
posture	Haltung, Körperhaltung

HOW TO USE

Pronouns

Anwendung:		
Pronomen sind sogenannte Fürwörter. Sie ersetzen ein Substantiv und vermeiden dadurch eine Wiederholung des gleichen Wortes in einem Satz.		The lorry was late, **it** had been delayed.
Arten von Pronomen:		
1. **hinweisende** Fürwörter (Demonstrativpronomen)		this, that, these, those Example: **These** letters were inquiries, **those** are offers.
2. Fürwörter, die **am Anfang von Nebensätzen** stehen (Relativpronomen)		who, whose, which, that, whoever Example: It was the first phone call **that** I received this morning.
3. **fragende** Fürwörter (Interrogativpronomen)		who, what, where Example: **Who** did you send for?
4. **persönliche** Fürwörter (Personalpronomen), drei Arten:		
Subjektpronomen	Objektpronomen	Possessivpronomen
Example: **I** like to drive a forklift.	Example: My girlfriend loves **me** but not **him**.	Example: This safety helmet is **mine**.
I	me	mine
you	you	yours
he/she/it	him/her/it	his/her/its
we	us	ours
you	you	yours
they	them	theirs

2.3.4. EXERCISE

Fill the gaps with the correct pronoun.

1. My name is Paul. (1) I am German. My mother's name is Ellen. (2) She is from Ireland. Karl is my dad. (3) He is an office clerk.
2. Our manager would like my colleague or (4) me to ring up the customer. My best friends live far away. (5) They sometimes visit me.
3. Susan and Carol started their apprenticeship last month. Paul left the warehouse earlier with (6) them .

4. Did you or (7) ______ speak with the purchasing department?
5. Carol wants to get a driver's license next year. The workbook is for (8) her .
6. Here is another invoice. I don't know what to do with (9) it .
7. My friends and I love ice cream. These ice lollies are for (10) them .

2.3.5. EXERCISE

Fill the gaps either with "who" or "which".

1. The driver came with another colleague (1) who waited inside the lorry.
2. My colleague (2) who worked at the goods receipt had an accident.
3. Give me the delivery note (3) which is in the office, please.
4. A warehouse operator is a person (4) who works in a store room.
5. Did you take the forklift truck (5) which was outside the warehouse?
6. Thank you very much for your leaflet (6) which was very interesting.
7. I do not know the name of the colleague (7) who told me to unload the goods.

2.4. Safety Signs and Safety Clothing

2.4.1. MATCHING

Match the safety signs with the English expressions.

Prohibition signs	Fire safety signs	Emergency signs	Hazard warning signs	Mandatory signs

The safe way. Where to go in an emergency.	Location where you can find fire equipment.	You must do. Carry out the action given by the sign.	Caution. Risk of danger. Hazard ahead.	Stop. Do not. You must not.

2

2.4.2. MATCHING

Match the expressions to the corresponding symbols.

forklifts in operation | emergency meeting point | fire extinguisher | fire hose | first aid station | floating load | hearing and eye protection must be worn | no admittance | no storage or stacking | wear safety gloves

hearing and eye protection

emergency meeting point

fire extinguisher

forklifts in operation

first aid station

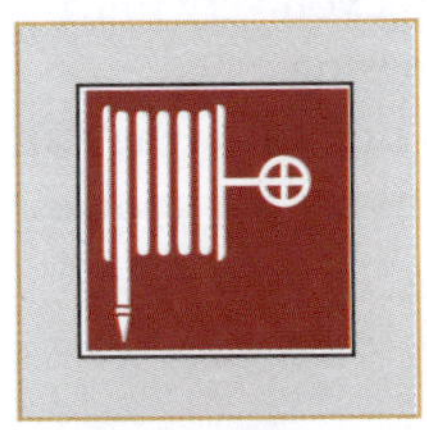

fire hose

no storage or stacking

no admittance

floating load

wear safety gloves

2.4.3. WRITING

Describe the five types of safety signs with the words and phrases in the box.

Colours:	red and black on white | black on yellow | white on red | white on green | white on blue
Shape:	a circle | a triangle | a square | circular band with diagonal cross bar
Meaning:	prohibition | danger | alarm | warning | emergency escape | first aid | no danger | fire-fighting equipment | mandatory
Instructions:	specific behaviour or action | be careful | take precautions | dangerous | behaviour | stop | identification and location | doors | exits

2.4.4. MATCHING

Match the elements of the personal protective equipment with the pictures.

ear protection | goggles | safety boots with anti-slip sole | safety helmet | safety vest | skin protection | weather protective clothing | work gloves | work trousers

2.5. Business Correspondence – E-Mails and Business Letters

2.5.1. BRAINSTORMING

Brainstorm with your neighbour how a buyer can find information about goods and suppliers. Make a list of information sources and present your findings to the class.

2.5.2. ANALYSING

Galaton is a supplier of safety equipment. Have a look at the company's website and answer the questions.

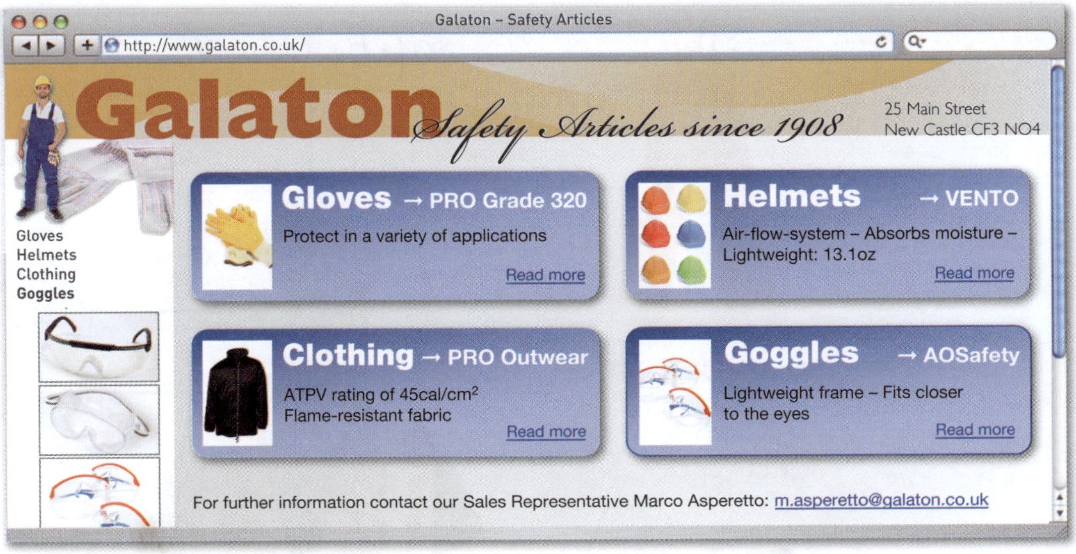

1. Where is the company located?

It's located in 25 Main Str. in New Castle.

2. Which products do they offer?

They offer gloves, helmets, clothing and goggles.

3. Who do you have to contact for more details?

You have to contact their sales representative

2.5.3. MATCHING

Ronald Hensten of *Hensten Electrics* writes an e-mail to the sales representative of *Galaton.*

a. Match the numbered parts of the e-mail to the typical elements of an e-mail message.
b. Copy the list of elements of an e-mail message into your exercise book. Use a dictionary to translate them into German.

From:	rhensten@electrics.co.uk	❶
To:	M.asperetto@galaton.co.uk	❷
Date:	10 October 20__	❸
Subject:	Interest in safety equipment	❹

Dear Mr Asperetto ❺

I visited your website and found your range of safety articles very interesting.

We are a medium-sized company in the electric industry and are particularly interested in a large number of goggles and gloves for our electricians.

Could you please send us a catalogue and price list including terms of delivery and payment? Do you grant quantity discounts on large orders?

We would be pleased to receive a sample of the goggles AOSafety and the gloves ProGrade. ❻

We look forward to hearing from you soon. ❼

Yours sincerely ❽

Ronald Hensten ❾
HENSTEN ELECTRICS
48 Golden Road Manchester M11 4NS
Phone 01234 5678 Email: rhensten@electrics.co.uk ❿
www.hensten-electrics.co.uk

2	recipient's e-mail address	7	complimentary close
	Bcc – blind carbon copy	9	sender's full name
5	salutation		sender's position
1	sender's e-mail address		Cc – carbon copy
10	footer (company name, address etc.)	6	message
4	subject	8	goodwill phrase
3	date		attachment

c. There are four items left in the list above. Discuss when and where they are used in an e-mail.

2.5.4. MATCHING

Mr Hensten is in urgent need of safety gloves and goggles. As he has technical problems with his e-mail system, he decides to send a business letter to Mr Asperetto by snail mail. Complete the list below by matching the English parts of the business letter to their German translations.

Hensten Electrics

48 Golden Road Manchester M11 4NS
Phone 01234 5678
Email: hensten@electrics.co.uk — **1. letterhead**

Our ref.: P/rh — **2. reference line**

15 October 20__ — **3. date**

Mr Marco Asperetto
GALATON
25 Main Street
New Castle
CF3 NO4 — **4. recipient's address**

Dear Mr Asperetto — **5. salutation**

Safety articles — **6. subject line**

I visited your website and found your range of safety articles very interesting.

We are a medium-sized company in the electric industry and are particularly interested in a large number of goggles and gloves for our electricians. — **7. body of the letter**

Could you please send us a catalogue and price list including terms of delivery and payment. Do you grant quantity discounts on large orders?

We would be pleased to receive a sample of the goggles AOSafety and of the gloves ProGrade.

We look forward to your early reply.

Yours sincerely — **8. complimentary close**

Ronald Hensten
Ronald Hensten
Manager — **9. signature block**

Empfängeradresse	~~letterhead~~ recipients address	Anrede	salutation
Unterschrift	signature bloch	Datum	date
Bezugszeichenzeile	reference line	Grußformel	complimentary close
Betreff	subject line	Brieftext	body of the letter
Briefkopf	letterhead		

2.5.5. ANALYSING

Now look at the parts of the e-mail on page 37 and find out the differences between the structure of an e-mail and the layout of a business letter. Discuss with your classmates.

SKILLS

Useful tips for an appropriate style in business correspondence

- Express your ideas politely. Use words like "thanks", "please" and "would" or "could".
- Choose one-word constructions instead of phrasal verbs (to give back, to return, to fill in, to complete).
- Do not use capital letters – capitalising sounds like shouting at someone.
- Do not use abbreviations or contractions, write everything out in full, e. g. not "it's" but "it is".
- Do not use emoticons or text message abbreviations.

2.5.6. MATCHING

Rephrase the sentences 1 to 10 by using the formal sentences a. to j.

e	1. I saw your goods on your website.
a	2. Send me a pricelist with terms of payment.
h	3. I need the information now.
b	4. When can you deliver?
d	5. Can I get a discount?
f	6. We await your reply immediately.
i	7. The stuff was damaged.
g	8. The guy at your stand gave me a catalogue.
j	9. This is poor quality.
c	10. I'll order more articles if they are good.

a. Could you please send us your pricelist including terms of payment.
b. Please let me have your earliest delivery date.
c. If the articles sell well, we will place a substantial order.
d. Do you grant any discounts?
e. I have visited your website and found your products interesting.
f. We look forward to your early reply.
g. I visited your stand at the trade fair where I obtained a catalogue of your products.
h. We would be grateful to receive the information as soon as possible.
i. Unfortunately, the products arrived in bad condition.
j. We regret to inform you that the quality of the product does not meet our requirements.

WORD BANK

delivery date	Liefertermin
discount	Rabatt, Ermäßigung
to grant	gewähren, einräumen
grateful	dankbar
range of	Auswahl/Angebot an
to rephrase	umformulieren
requirement	Anforderung
substantial	umfangreich, beträchtlich
terms of delivery	Lieferbedingungen
terms of payment	Zahlungsbedingungen

2.5.7. CROSSWORD PUZZLE

Complete the crossword puzzle.

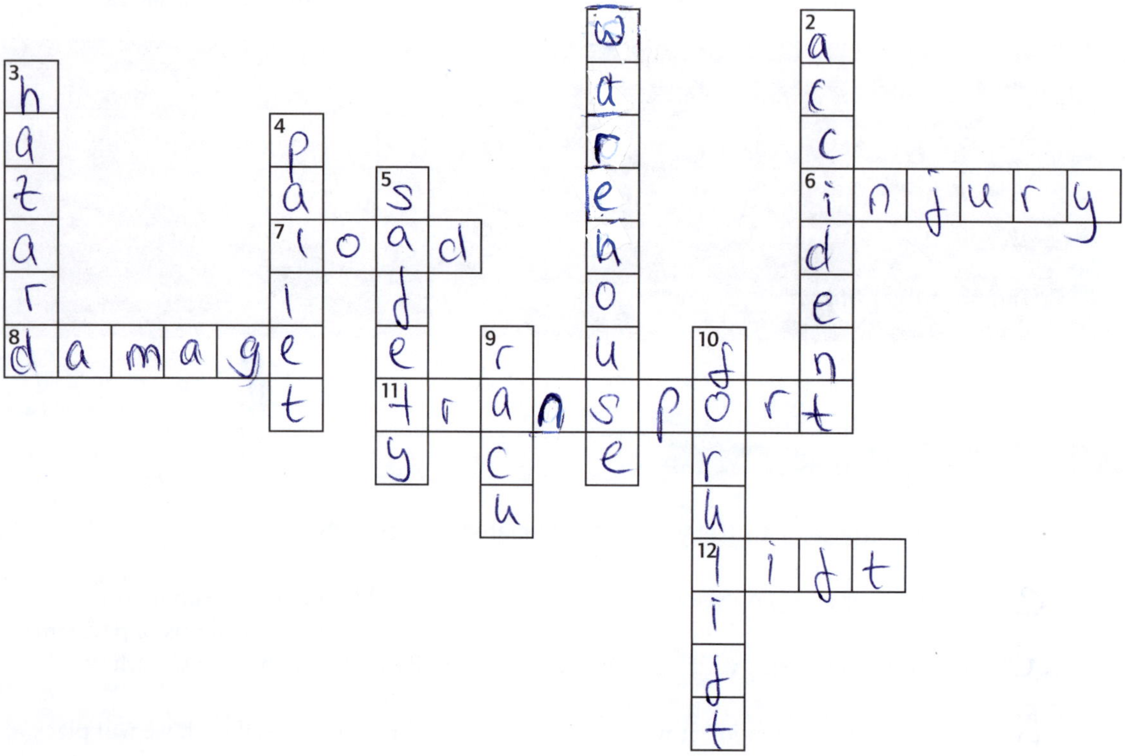

DOWN

1. Lager
2. Unfall
3. Gefahr
4. Palette
5. Sicherheit
9. Regal
10. Gabelstapler

ACROSS

6. Verletzung
7. beladen
8. beschädigen
11. transportieren
12. anheben

3 Receiving and Storing Goods

DISCUSSION

Look at the picture and describe what you see.

BRAINSTORMING

What do you or your colleagues do when your company receives a delivery? Exchange your experience with your neighbour and make a mind map from your results together. Put your mind map on a poster and prepare a short presentation. You may use the vocabulary from the box below. Decide who is going to present which part.

~~unload lorry~~ | ~~check/sign~~ | ~~delivery note~~ | ~~count boxes~~ | ~~check on damages~~ | ~~compare delivery with order~~ | ~~put goods on pallets~~

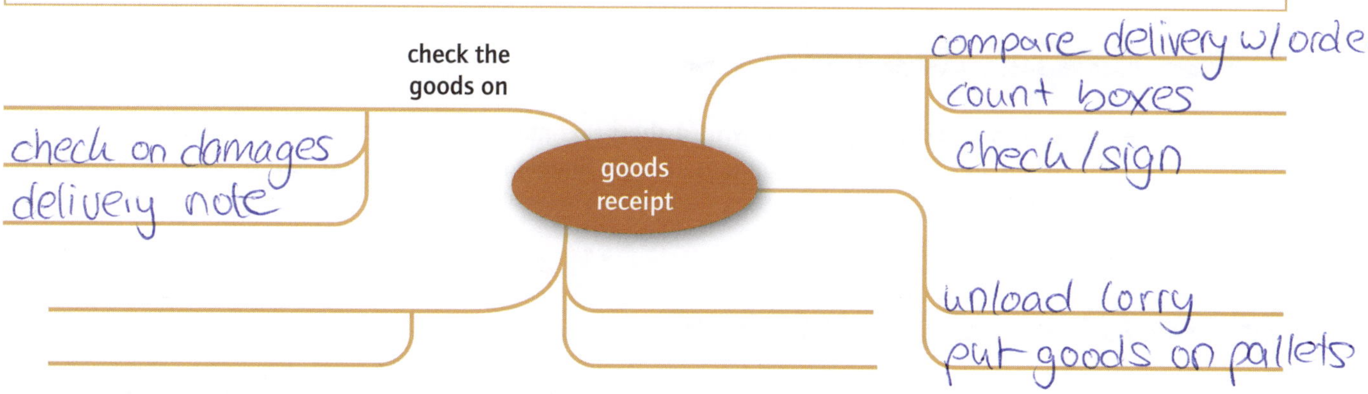

PRESENTATION

Present your mind map to the class. Try to speak in complete sentences and keep eye contact with the class and the teacher.

3

3.1. Receiving Goods

3.1.1. ANALYSING

a. There are different activities in the goods receiving department. Bring them into the correct order.
b. Add the German translations.

a.		b.
☐	check reusable packages	wiederverwendbare Verpackungen prüfen
☐	sign delivery note	Lieferschein unterschreiben
☐	count amount of packages	Menge der Lieferung zählen
☐	inform purchasing department about noticed transport damages	den Einkauf über Transport-schäden informieren
☐	unload goods	Güter entladen
☐	delivery of goods	Warenlieferung
☐	check condition of packages	Zustand der Verpackung prüfen
☐	incoming goods inspection	Wareneingangskontrolle
☐	document noticed transport damages	Transportschäden dokumentieren
☐	exchange reusable packages	wiederverwendbare Packungen tauschen
☐	check address	Adresse prüfen

3.1.2. WRITING

Look at the chart again and write a short text about what warehouse operators have to do when they receive a consignment. Use the Simple Present and read your text to the class afterwards.

3.1.3. LISTENING FOR GIST

Listen carefully to the report on how goods have to be checked appropriately. Write down which four categories are checked by the warehouse staff.

3.1.4. LISTENING FOR DETAIL

Listen again and answer the following questions.

1. How do you check the identity of the goods?

   You must compare the delivery note with ____________________

2. How can you ascertain the quantity of goods?

   ____

3. What do you compare if you want to check the quality?

   ____

4. What does the term "goods delivered in apparently good condition" mean?

   ____

5. Name four documents the quality control department or the warehouse staff need for the check.

   ____

   ____

6. What do you enter into the stock list?

   ____

   ____

SKILLS

Listening for gist
Listening for gist means that it is not necessary to understand everything. You should merely try to get the core message. Do not get frustrated or demotivated if you are not able to identify all the words.

WORD BANK

apparently	anscheinend, augenscheinlich
to check	prüfen
condition	Zustand
delivery note	Lieferschein
to document	beurkunden, dokumentieren
to exchange sth.	etwas austauschen
offer	Angebot
order	Auftrag
purchasing department	Einkaufsabteilung
reusable	wieder verwendbar, Mehrweg…
to sign a receipt	eine Quittung unterschreiben
stock list	Lagerliste
to unload sth.	etwas abladen

3.1.5. READING

Read the text you have just listened to. With your neighbour, decide if the statements below the text are true (T) or false (F). If they are false, correct them.

Goods Receipt

As the warehouse is the **interface** between several departments it is very important to have good warehouse management with well-organised processes and procedures. The requirements of modern logistics are demanding and complex. Every day a lot of **consignments** arrive in various companies. Before the goods can be stored properly the **delivery** has to be checked by the goods receiving department. This part of the procedure is called "Goods Receipt". The warehouse operators inspect the incoming goods. The goods are registered here and locations are found before the articles are put **in stock**. In small companies there is often no goods receiving department and all the work is done by the normal warehouse staff, but in larger firms a separate department is recommended.

After the goods are unloaded the buyer has to check the delivery. For checking the identity you have to compare the delivery note with the contents of the packages. By counting the articles or packages you can find out if the amount is correct or not. Before the buyer opens the packages he inspects the condition of the shipment and checks that there is no visible damage. If everything looks alright, he signs a copy of the delivery note with the expression "goods delivered in apparently good condition". He has to do that while the carrier is still present. Later the buyer checks the quality of the goods which is far more difficult. He has to check if the quality **corresponds to** what was ordered. He compares the **order** and the **offer** with the **packing list** and the **delivery note** and other **forwarding documents** such as the **waybill** and the **air waybill**.

It is also very important to compare the offer with the **invoice** because the prices in the invoice must be identical to the prices in the offer. If everything is acceptable you enter the goods into the **stock list**. For this you enter the article number and the quantity that has arrived. As mentioned above, the buyer has to complain directly to the **carrier** in the case of any visible damage. Damaged goods or goods which have not been ordered have to be kept until the supplier gives instructions what to do with them. The supplier has to be informed about any hidden damage or other mistakes directly after detection without delay. In many companies several departments for example purchasing, **accounting** or production are informed about the arrived goods by a **goods receipt slip**. This can be a paper form or a data set.

true (=T) or false (=F)

1. Every company must have a "Goods Receiving Department".
2. You have to check the condition of the packages the day after the receipt of goods at the latest.
3. You have to keep faulty items in your company and wait for the supplier's directive.
4. Damages which aren't visible at first sight can be complained about within certain time limits.
5. A ten percent price difference between the offer and the invoice has to be accepted.

3.1.6. VOCABULARY WORK

complain | consignment | damage | delivery note | offer | in stock | order

Fill in the gaps with a word from the box above.

1. The supplier will send us the (1) consignment ______ tomorrow. We will check it and decide if we order a large amount.
2. The ordered goods from our supplier will probably arrive next week. UPS will deliver the (2) order ______ to our company.
3. I always compare the (3) delivery note ______ with the order.
4. I don't know if we have enough articles (4) in stock ______.
5. There are some packages with an obvious (5) damage ______. We will complain about that immediately.
6. If the offer is very good we will place a larger (6) ______.
7. If there is a damage we will have to (7) complain ______.

3.1.7. MEDIATION

Your manager has asked you to do a short training course for a new trainee about the duties of the buyer. He has asked you to mediate this text into German because the trainee doesn't speak any English.

Complaints

It is very important to complain about a damage to the supplier and/or the carrier without delay. If both contract partners are business people, the buyer has to inspect the goods immediately and claim visible damages at once. A hidden damage must be complained about directly after detection, but not later than two years after delivery. Otherwise the buyer would lose his right against the supplier unless the supplier hasn't mentioned a damage he knows about on purpose.

WORD BANK

accounting	Buchhaltung
air waybill	Luftfrachtbrief
carrier	Frachtführer
to complain about	reklamieren, sich über etwas beschweren
consignment / delivery / shipment	Lieferung
to correspond to	etwas entsprechen
forwarding documents	Warenbegleitpapiere
goods receipt slip	Wareneingangsschein
invoice	Rechnung
interface	Schnittstelle
in stock	auf Lager, vorrätig
packing list	Packliste
quality control	Qualitätskontrolle

HOW TO USE — Will-Future

Anwendung:		
– um Vorhersagen oder Vermutungen auszudrücken		The prices **will** rise next year.
– für spontane Absichtserklärungen		Are you busy? I **will** help you.
– für Versprechen		I **will** load the lorry later.
Bildung: Will-Future = "will" + Verb		
Positive Aussage	**Verneinung**	**Frage**
I/you/he/she/it/we/you/they will read Kurzform: …'ll read	I/you/he/she/it/we/you/they will not read Kurzform: …won't read	Will I/you/he/she/it/we/you/they read?

3.1.8. EXERCISE

Fill in the correct form of the Will-Future.

1. The weather tomorrow (1) will be (be) warm und sunny. There (2) won't be (not be) any rain.
2. My colleague said: "I (3) will help (help) you with the lorry."
3. I think our company (4) won't take (not take) a new apprentice next year because our sales figures are not very good.
4. My brother offered yesterday: "I (5) will pick you up (pick you up) after work."
5. Maybe the next consignment (6) will arrive (arrive) next week.
6. I think my boss (7) won't install (not install) the new software before Monday.
7. We all hope that our economy (8) won't get (not get) worse again.
8. The new unemployment rate (9) will be published (be published) in November.
9. Our customer (10) will be (be) very disappointed because you have forgotten to inform him about the delay.
10. I'm afraid my boss (11) won't give (not give) me a week off in July. We have a lot of work in July.

3.2. Registration of Goods Receipt

Goods Receipt Slip

Hensten Electrics

Number	85652/8	Date	❶ 20..-12-08
	20..-12-08	Time	14:35
		User	Smith

Order number	❷ 125665	Supplier ❸	Homag Ltd.
Delivery note number	7852/96		Liverpool
Invoice number	204588		

Article ❹ M_8_x_30 — 300 units ❺

Raised countersunk M 8 x 30 according to DIN 966
Recessed head H,4,8 zinc-plated ❻

Version	12/36
Charge number	233
Storage bin ❼	B/135
Cost centre	002

36/658

3.2.1. MATCHING

Look at the form. Fill in the gaps below to match the English and German expressions with the numbers in the form.

	German	English
❶	Datum	date
❷	Bestellnummer	order number
❸	Verkäufer	supplier
❹	Artikelnummer	article number
❺	Menge	amount
❻	Artikelbeschreibung	article description
❼	Lagereinheit	storage bin

3.2.2. BRAINSTORMING

Work in pairs. Which information does a goods receipt slip need to contain? Which departments need a copy and why? Write your ideas on cards. Use different colours for the pieces of information and the departments.
Pin your cards with ideas from your pair work on the two posters when your teacher asks you to. If your idea is already there, give your card back to your teacher.

3.2.3. WRITING

Write a text about the goods receipt slip and its importance for the company. You can use the ideas from the posters. Read your text to the class afterwards.

HOW TO USE **If-Clauses, Type I**

Bedingungssätze (If-Clauses) bestehen aus einem if-Satz und einem Hauptsatz:	
Der **if-Satz** nennt eine realistische Bedingung: etwas, das eintreten kann, soll oder wird. Bildung: **Simple Present**	**If** we **work** on Saturday, (Wenn wir am Samstag arbeiten,
Der **Hauptsatz** drückt aus, was passiert, wenn die Bedingung erfüllt ist. Bildung: **will / can / must + Infinitiv**	we **will finish** this order next week. werden wir diesen Auftrag in der nächsten Woche beenden.)
Achtung: – if-Satz kann vor oder nach dem Hauptsatz stehen – niemals „will" im if-Satz verwenden	

3.2.4. EXERCISE

Choose the correct word(s) underlined in each sentence.

1. If you ring/will ring this bell, the receptionist will come.
2. If you take your umbrella with you tomorrow, you aren't/won't get wet.
3. My mother will go to bed early if she will feel/feels tired.
4. The customer will call/is called later if the delivery doesn't arrive on time.
5. If it rains/will rain tomorrow, we won't load the lorry.
6. If you don't hurry/won't hurry up, we won't reach the plane.
7. If our teacher is/will be ill tomorrow, we won't have an English lesson.
8. I will look/look up the word if you lend me your dictionary.
9. If you don't come/won't come to work tomorrow, your company will send you a warning letter.
10. If you get a third warning letter, your boss will fire/fires you.

3.2.5. EXERCISE

Fill in the correct form of the verb. Use the If-Clause, Type I.

1. If it (1) rains (rain) tomorrow, we (2) won't be able (not be able) to load the lorry.
2. If we (3) don't order (not order) the new items next week, our customers (4) will have to (have to) wait.
3. All the apprentices (5) will receive (receive) a bonus if they (6) will execute (execute) the orders on time.
4. My teacher (7) will give (give) me a good mark if I (8) am (be) active in his lessons the coming weeks.
5. If you (9) don't hurry (not hurry) up, you (10) will miss (miss) the bus.
6. If the new colleague (11) doesn't enter (not enter) the article into the stock list, it (12) will be (be) difficult to know what we have in stock.
7. If the taxi (13) doesn't come (not come) soon, we (14) will miss (miss) our plane.
8. What (15) will you do (do) if your boss (16) won't let (not let) you take a day off?
9. I (17) will give (give) you a lift if your car (18) is (be) still at the garage after work.
10. I (19) will phone (phone) our customers if the delivery (20) is (be) late.

3.2.6. INTERNET RESEARCH

There are three main ways to register the goods which have been received. Search the Internet and inform yourself about one of these ways. Prepare a short presentation in English. Think carefully which technical equipment you need for your presentation and ask your teacher to make sure that the equipment is available.

1. Barcode or label (1-D-Codes and 2-D-Codes)
2. Serial Shipping Container Code (SSCC)
3. Radio Frequency Identification (RFID)

4 012345 987652

SKILLS

If you have to do an Internet research, the following tips might be useful for you:
1. Think about the search words carefully.
2. Do not only work with one source and cross-check each piece of information.
3. Wikipedia is always a good start because it gives you an overview about the topic and useful links at the end.
4. Use only original, reliable sources and not texts which are only based on them.

3.3. Storing Goods

3.3.1. MATCHING

Match the following articles and their need for protection and write them into the correspon-ding column.

dairy products | flower soil | fruit and vegetables | grain | paper | technical devices | textiles

Protection against	Examples
sunlight	
loss of taste	
humidity	
vermin	
heat/cold	
drying up	

3.3.2. READING

Read the following text about the proper storage of goods and answer the questions below the text.

Storing Goods under Appropriate Conditions

There are many aspects to **consider** if you want to store the delivered goods **appropriately**. It is not sufficient to keep the warehouse tidy and **well-arranged**. Different goods require different storage. Milk, cheese and butter for example must be **protected from** heat whereas tobacco products must be kept warm and dry. Wrong **treatment** or handling can cause serious damages that are often expensive or even dangerous. Therefore a lot of rules have to be **followed** and warning signs are put up to **prevent** damages, accidents, fires etc.

Warehouse operators know the best conditions for their products and take measures against heat, cold and other conditions which are not **favourable** for the stored goods. As the employers are responsible for the safety of people and the goods in the warehouse they hand out instructions their staff have to sign and follow. But there are also handling signs on many packages to show how to handle them properly.

The symbols for package handling instructions are internationally standardized in ISO R/780 (International Organization for Standardization) and in DIN 55 402 (DIN, German Institute for Standardization). The symbols must never be **omitted** as they are self-explaining and so overcome language problems in international transport operations. Therefore, it is not difficult for new employees or apprentices to **gain** solid knowledge and experience about correct handling.

1. How does a proper warehouse have to be kept?

different goods require different storage

2. Which conditions products have to be prevented from are mentioned in the text?

dairy products must be protected from heat, tobacco needs to be kept worm and dry

3. Why is it so important to know which conditions are best for each product?

to prevent damages, accidents, fires, etc.

4. Why do the employees have to follow rules and safety instructions?

Because they're responsible for the safety of people and the goods

WORD BANK

appropriate	angemessen
by heart	auswendig
to consider	in Erwägung ziehen, betrachten
favourable	günstig
to gain	erlangen, aneignen
to follow rules/instructions	Regeln/Anweisungen befolgen
to omit	weglassen
to protect from	schützen vor
vermin	Schädlinge

3.3.3. MATCHING

Match the symbols and their meaning.

do not use forklift truck here | fragile, handle with care | keep away from heat | keep dry | protect from heat and radioactive sources | tear off here | top | use no hooks

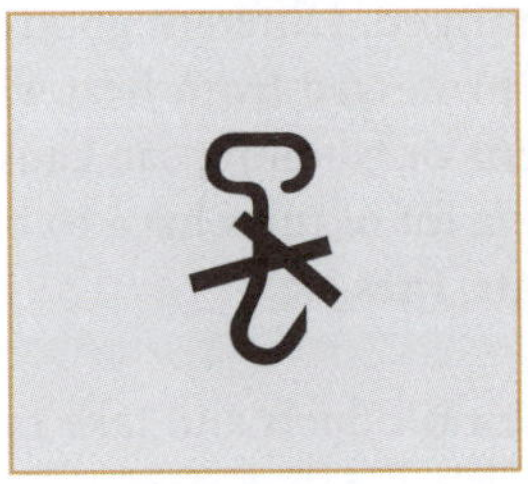

use no hooks

top

keep away from heat

protect from heat and radioactive sources

fragile, handle with care

keep dry

do not use fork-lift truck here

tear off here

3.4. Proper Storage

3.4.1. MATCHING

Work with your neighbour and read the little text below. Match the pictures and the corresponding words on the next page. Talk with your neighbour about the types of storage you have in your company. Make a list with the articles you store in different ways and report to the class afterwards.

Storage Types

The appropriate storage of each item on stock is difficult and totally depends on the nature of the article, the type of the company, the location of the stock, the owner of the product and many further aspects. That's why you can distinguish the storage types in various ways. There are, for example, different sorts of racking systems like flat or high-rise storage as well as central or local and open or closed storage.

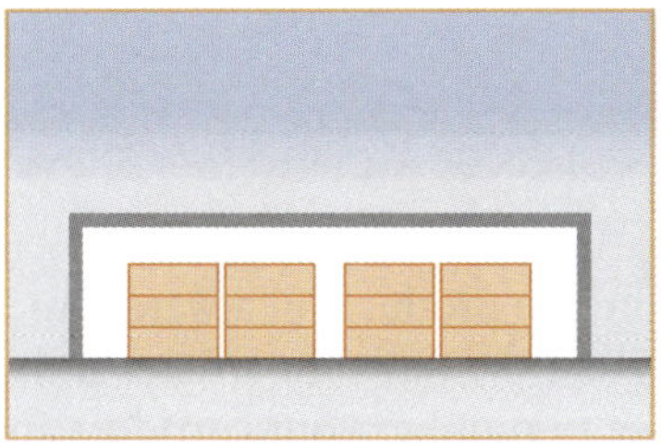

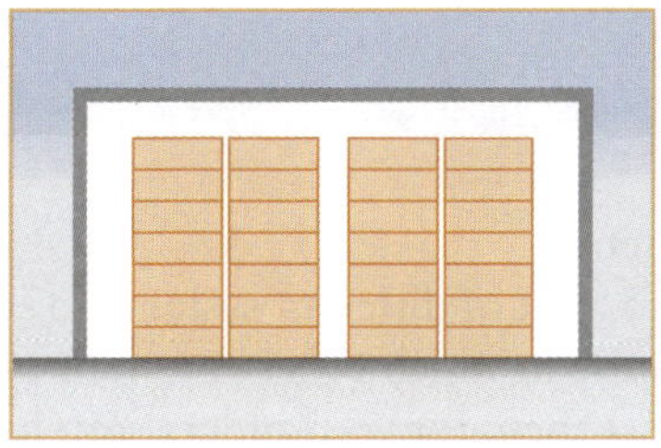

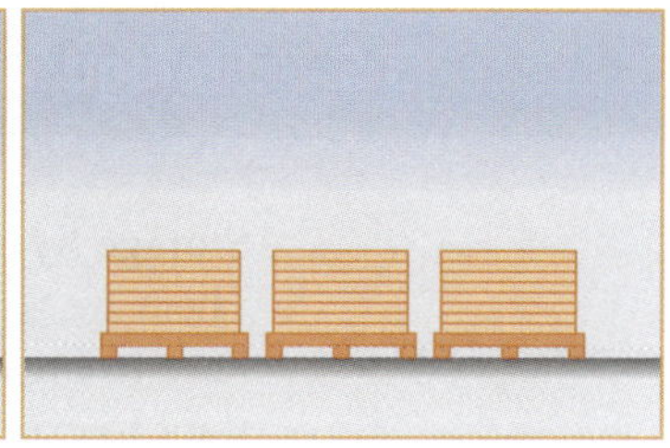

flat-rise storage | high-rise storage | open storage

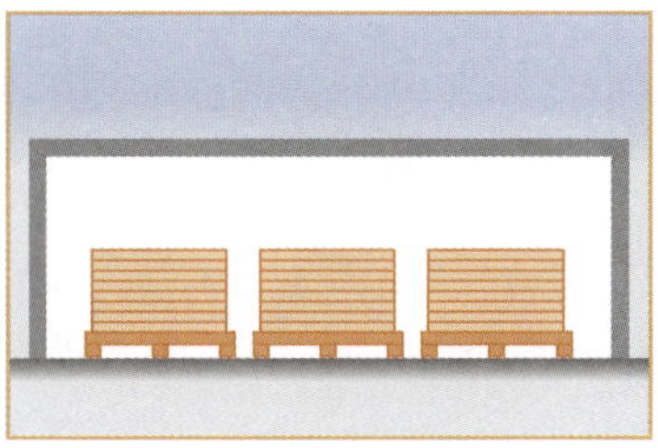

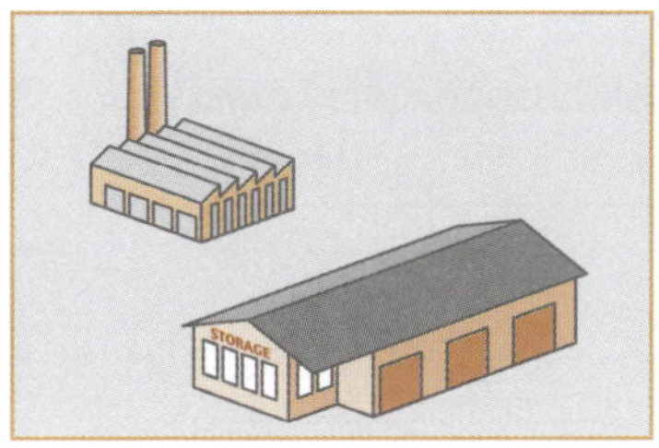

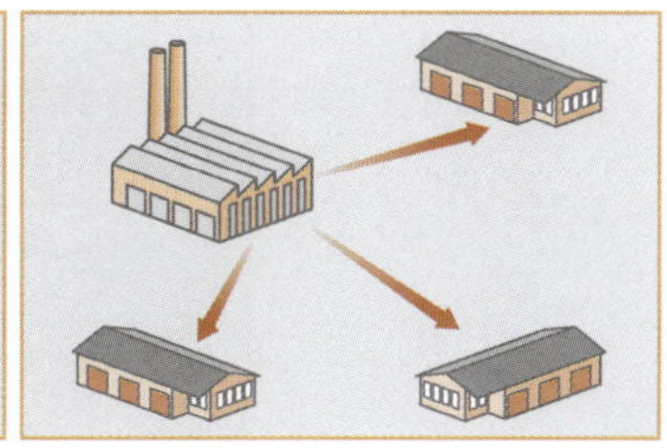

closed storage | central storage | local storage

3.4.2. BRAINSTORMING

Many big companies have fully automatic warehouse equipment like conveyor belts, packing stations etc. that works non-stop. This only makes sense if it is used continuously and the process is standardised.

What are the advantages and the disadvantages of this modern technology for a company and for the employees? Brainstorm and collect your ideas on the board or the OHP.

3.4.3. WRITING

Write a short text about the advantages and disadvantages of fully automatic warehouse equipment. Use the phrases in the word bank below and evaluate the technology through the eyes of both the employer and the employees. Finish your text with a personal conclusion.

WORD BANK

as a result	schlussfolgernd
first of all	zuerst, zuallererst
furthermore	außerdem, darüber hinaus
in addition	ergänzend, hinzu kommt
in my opinion	meiner Meinung nach
last but not least	nicht zuletzt
on the one hand, on the other hand	auf der einen Seite, auf der anderen Seite
therefore	somit, deshalb
to sum it up	um es zusammenzufassen
whereas	wobei, wohingegen
while	während

3.5. Storage Systems

Storage Systems

There are also a lot of different systems to store the products in a warehouse. But first of all you have to organise in which order you want to store the different articles and in which order you want to extract them for your orders. You have to number your corridors and aisles so that you will be able to find each item immediately. It is also important to store the goods in a way that the employees always have the shortest way possible.

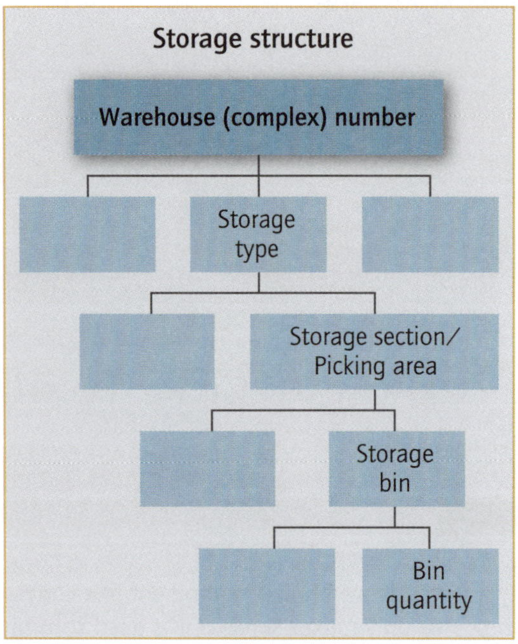

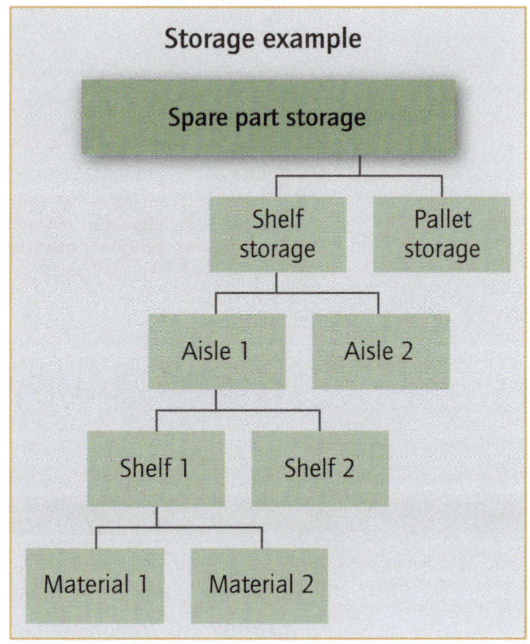

3.5.1. PRESENTATION

a. Form groups of four or five students and take one topic from the following list. Tell your teacher which topic you have chosen. Inform yourselves about the topic and prepare a presentation about it.

1. GTIN-13 (former EAN)
2. ISBN-13-Code
3. Organisation of shelves
4. FIFO
5. LIFO
6. HIFO
7. Storage zones

b. Present your topic to the class. Ask your teacher which technical equipment you can use and make sure that everything works before you start your presentation.

3.6. Hazardous Goods

3.6.1. MATCHING

For the handling of dangerous or hazardous goods a worldwide standardised system (GHS) has been developed. It consists of nine pictograms. Look up the following words on the Internet or in your dictionary and write the correct expression under each symbol.

compressed gas | corrosive | dangerous to the environment | explosive | flammable | may cause cancer or genetic defects | oxidizing | toxic | warning

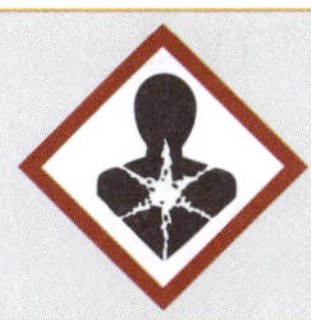

may cause cancer or genetic defects

flammable

toxic

warning

corrosive

dangerous to the environment

explosive

compressed gas

oxidizing

3.6.2. MEDIATION

Your boss has given you the following text in German and has asked you to translate it into English for the trainee from England. Use the vocabulary from the box below.

Das Arbeiten im Lager kann manchmal gefährlich sein. Deshalb muss jeder Arbeitgeber seinen Mitarbeitern auf einfache und verständliche Art erklären, wie sie mit gefährlichen Gütern arbeiten müssen. Außerdem müssen Warntafeln im Lager die Gefahrensymbole erklären. Ferner muss der Arbeitgeber erklären, wie die Mitarbeiter sich im Gefahrenfall verhalten sollen und wie man erste Hilfe leisten kann. Abschließend muss er zeigen, wie man Abfälle richtig entsorgt.

to dispose of waste | to give first aid | in an easy and understandable way | in case of danger

3.7. Business Correspondence – Enquiries

3.7.1. READING

Read the following text about the definition of an enquiry and complete it with the words from the box.

~~brochure~~ | ~~discounts~~ | ~~nature~~ | prospective | ~~payment~~ | ~~presentation~~ | ~~price~~ | ~~request~~ | ~~terms~~

In a business context, an enquiry is a (1) request for information. Before ordering goods or services, the (2) prospective customer is likely to require details about the goods in question. An important piece of information for the buyer is the (3) price of the goods and the (4) nature which the seller will be able to supply at. There are many questions to be clarified: Is the supplier in a position to grant (5) discounts e. g. on large orders? What are the (6) terms of delivery? Which terms of (7) payment are applied?
Additionally, the buyer may ask for a catalogue or a (8) brochure and sometimes for samples of the goods. For specific goods, it might be necessary to arrange for a demonstration or (9) ~~prospective~~ presentation on the buyer's premises.

3.7.2. MATCHING

Match the following words from the list to their German translation.

c	1. nature of the goods/service	a. Preis
a	2. price	b. Rabatt/Nachlass
b	3. discount	c. Beschaffenheit der Ware/Dienstleistung
f	4. terms of delivery	d. Lieferzeitpunkt
e	5. terms of payment	e. Zahlungsbedingungen
d	6. delivery time	f. Lieferbedingungen

3.7.3. READING

Read the enquiry for ratchet straps and answer the questions below.

FRESHLINE Ltd.

25 Benton Road * New Castle NE27 6RU
Phone 0191 232 4233 • Fax: 0191 221 0138
E-Mail: freshline@food.co.uk
www.freshline-food.co.uk

Our ref.: RS-str
08 October 20__

GTF Cargo Control Ltd.
199 Broughton Road Oxford Street
Edinburgh
EH7 4LN

Dear Sir or Madam

I refer to your advertisement in the latest issue of Business Magazine which has drawn our attention to your products.

We are a large company specialising in food production for the catering industry. For the transport of our freshly produced food we are looking for reliable loading equipment. We are particularly interested in your new Heavy Duty Ratchet Straps.

Could you please send us general information including technical data on the above mentioned lashing equipment. We would be pleased to receive a brochure including prices and terms of delivery and payment. Please let us know if you grant quantity discounts on substantial orders.

We look forward to hearing from you soon.

Yours faithfully

Peter Straw

Peter Straw

1. **Where did Mr Straw find out about *GTF Cargo Control Ltd.?***

He found it as an advertisement in the Business Magazine.

2. **What does he want them to send him?**

He wants general information about the lashing equipment

3. **Which elements of a business letter are missing?**

3.7.4. WRITING

You work for *Atlas Products*, a medium-sized company located in 13 Edward Court, London HA1 8NY. Your company is in urgent need of pallets for the warehouse. On *Wesco's* website you saw that they offer a new type of plastic pallets.
Write an enquiry to *Wesco & Sons*, 104 Stratford Avenue, Liverpool AB3 DE6:

- say how you learned about the company
- introduce your company
- ask for a catalogue and price list
- terms of delivery and delivery time
- say that you will place a substantial order if prices are competitive

HOW TO USE — Countable and Uncountable Nouns

Nomen können zählbar oder unzählbar sein:	
– **Zählbare Nomen** (countable nouns) bezeichnen Dinge, die man zählen kann. – Sie haben eine Singular- und eine Pluralform. – Das begleitende Verb steht entsprechend entweder im Singular oder im Plural.	one lorry – two lorries one pallet – two pallets one office – four offices The helmet **is** yellow. The helmets **are** yellow.
– **Unzählbare Nomen** (uncountable nouns) bezeichnen Dinge, die man nicht zählen kann. – Sie haben keine Pluralform. – Sie können nicht mit „a", „an" oder einem Zahlwort verwendet werden. – Das begleitende Verb steht immer im Singular. – Um Angaben über die Menge von unzählbaren Nomen zu machen, nennt man ein zählbares Nomen vorweg.	~~a~~ money ~~a~~ furniture ~~an~~ information ~~one~~ equipment The information about you **is** interesting. Our new safety equipment **is** very helpful. information – a piece of information data – two sets of data advice – a piece of advice
Achtung: – Manche Nomen sind im Deutschen zählbar, nicht aber in ihrer englischen Entsprechung.	It's interesting **work**. – Es ist **eine** interessante **Arbeit**. I've got good **news** for you. – Ich habe **eine** gute **Nachricht** für Sie.

3.7.5. EXERCISE

Fill the blanks with the words in brackets using "a" or "an" where necessary.

ACD Production was planning to redecorate their offices, therefore the manager was looking for (1) an information about (2) a new office furniture. On the Internet he saw (3) an advertisement for chairs, desks and filing cabinets. He clicked on the call-back button. The next day, the company's representative gave him (4) a call back. He was of (5) a great help to him on how to plan the renovation of the offices. Anne was searching for (6) ______ work. She went to the job agency where they gave her (7) a useful advice. Finally, they offered her (8) a job at the airport. She had enough (9) ______ experience in the travel business, so Anne got the job. Now she works at the check-in counter. Some people carry (10) ______ heavy luggage to the check-in point.

3.7.6. EXERCISE

Use the words from the box to make the nouns countable.

a bag of | ~~a bottle of~~ | ~~a cup of~~ | a kilo of | ~~a piece of~~ | a slice of

1. a cup of	coffee	6. a bottle of	mineral water
2. a bag of	luggage	7. a slice of	bread
3. a piece of	paper	8. ______	advice
4. a piece of	information	9. a piece of	furniture
5. a kilo of	potatoes	10. a slice of	cheese

WORD BANK

advice	Rat, Empfehlung
competitive	wettbewerbsfähig
delivery time	Lieferzeitpunkt, Lieferfrist
enquiry	Anfrage
filing cabinet	Aktenschrank
located	ansässig
luggage	Gepäck
medium-sized	mittelständisch
pallet	Palette
to redecorate	renovieren

3.7.7. CROSSWORD PUZZLE

Complete the crossword puzzle.

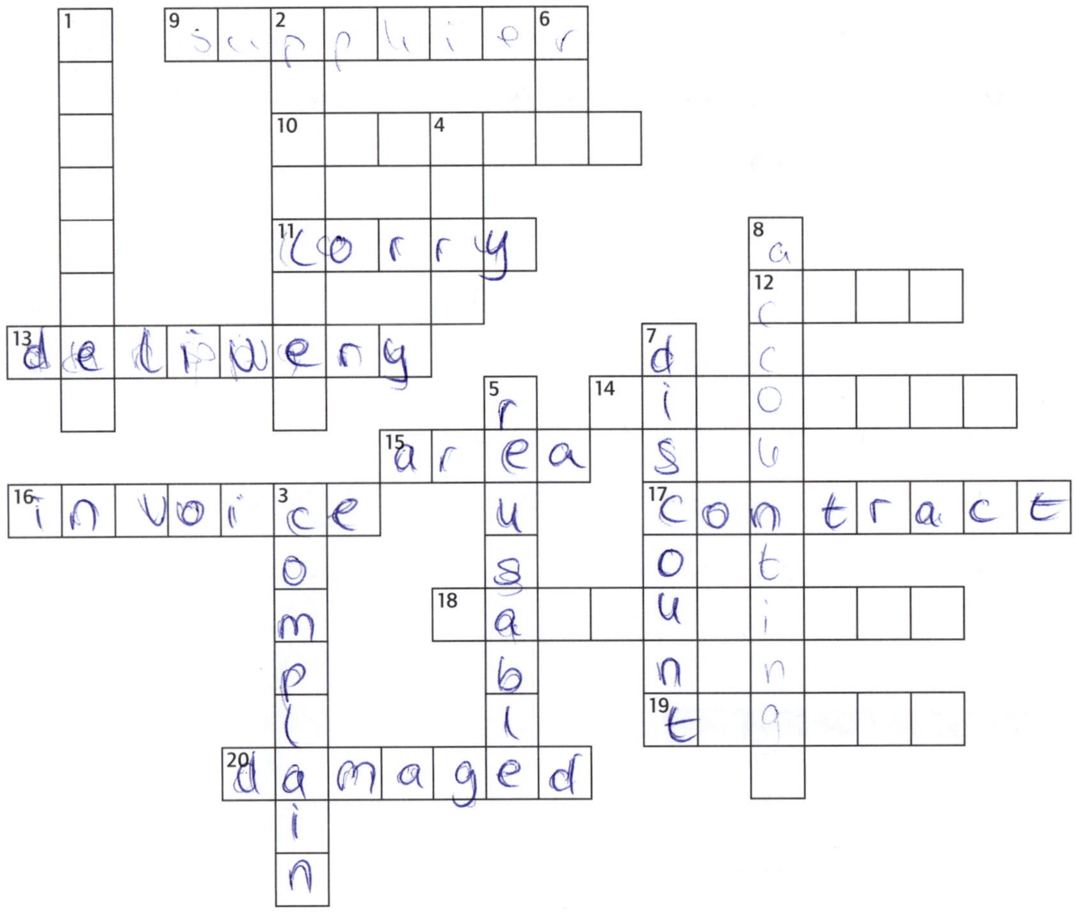

ACROSS

9. the company you deliver to
10. to take action that something does not happen
11. a big transport vehicle
12. to do something in order to make sure that everything is correct
13. another word for shipment
14. when things or people are very untidy ore disorganised
15. a particular part of a place, city or country
16. British word for bill
17. Our company signed a three year … with this supplier.
18. you store your goods under … conditions
19. a printed piece of paper that shows that you have paid to do something
20. not in good condition

DOWN

1. you take these when you want to store your goods properly
2. the company that delivers to you
3. to express dissatisfaction
4. it is not just urgent but it is … urgent
5. if you can use something again, it is …
6. I would like to … my own business.
7. reduction in the usual price of something
8. the colleagues who keep our financial records work in the …

4 Order Picking and Packing Goods

1

2

3

4

Order Picking

Order picking is one of a logistic warehouse's processes. Order picking means that the order-picker extracts a small number of goods from a warehousing system. The order picker has to deal with a number of independent customer orders. Picking processes have become an important part of the supply chain process. It is seen as the most labour-intensive and costly activity for almost every warehouse. The cost of order picking is estimated to be as much as 55 percent of the total warehouse operating expenses. There has been an increasing number of process improvements. They help companies to reduce costs and to meet the customer's needs.

DISCUSSION

Work together with your neighbour and answer the following questions.

a. If you look at the pictures above, what do you see?
b. Match the different methods of order picking to the pictures and describe them. Use the information in the text above and the words in the word bank from page 62.

(1) ______

(2) ______

(3) ______

(4) ______

c. Which method(s) do you use in your company? Explain to the class.

4

4.1. Order Picking

4.1.1. VOCABULARY WORK

Find words in the box below which fit these definitions or explanations.

customer | labour-intensive | order picker | order picking | supply chain | warehouse

a. extracting goods — order picking

b. person who extracts goods from a warehousing system — order picker

c. way from producer to the customer — supply chain

d. to whom goods are delivered — customer

e. where goods are stored — warehouse

f. is a lot of work — labour-intensive

4.1.2. DISCUSSION

To what extent will order picking be possible without the help of manpower in the future? Use the words in the word bank. Before starting a class discussion collect useful phrases like "in my opinion" or "on the one hand" etc. on the board.

WORD BANK

to become redundant	seinen Arbeitsplatz verlieren
(electronic) order picking	(beleglose) Kommissionierung
to decrease	fallen
to facilitate	erleichtern
to increase	steigen
logistics	Versorgung, Logistik
low level order picking	maschinengestützte Kommissionierung
pick-by-barcode	Kommisionieren per Strichcode
pick-by-light	Kommisionieren per LED-Anzeigen
pick-by-vision	Kommissionieren per Datenbrille
pick-by-voice	Kommissionieren per Sprachbefehl
order picking by pick list	beleghafte Kommissionierung
time consuming	zeitaufwändig

4.1.3. MATCHING

We can identify five main types of order picking. Match them with the definitions.

1. **picker to part method**
2. **sorting systems method**
3. **pick to box method**
4. **zone picking method**
5. **wave picking method**

a. Each order picker is assigned to one specific zone.
b. The order picker moves to collect the products necessary for several orders.
c. No movement of the order picker, the picking area is organized so that there are a number of picking stations connected by a conveyor. The order picker fills the box with the products from his station and the box moves to the other picking stations until the customer's order is complete.
d. The order picker moves to collect the products necessary for one order.
e. No movement of the order picker, the products are brought to him by an automatic system.

4.1.4. CREATIVE ACTIVITY

Chart a workflow of the "sorting systems method" and the "zone picking method" in your exercise book.

4.1.5. WRITING

What are the in-house and external reasons for extracting goods from a warehousing system? Match the pictures above with the keywords below and build complete sentences.

☐	sold out:	*The warehouse assistant extracts goods because the products are sold out.*
☐	annual stocktaking:	
☐	new product line:	
☐	seasonal sales:	
☐	assembly line:	

4.1.6. READING

Read the text carefully and decide if the statements below are true or false.

Toy Story

With over 1.2 million square feet of **storage area** and around 500 full-time employees, *Amethyst* operates from six distribution centres located in the heart of the UK. At its site in Wellesbourne, Warwickshire, *Amethyst* provides warehousing and distribution services to some of the toy industry's best known and most successful **brands**. At **peak periods**, such as in the run-up to Christmas, over 100 **trailers** a day arrive at the site. The **contents** of each incoming trailer are put into stock before orders are picked, packed and **dispatched** to retailers.

With low level order picking being an important part of the Wellesbourne operation, **articulated forklift trucks** represented the optimum handling solution. Because of its design, the articulated truck is perfectly suited to working in narrow **aisles** alongside order picking staff without creating a health and safety issue.

Once picked, the orders are held in a certain aisle where any relevant predelivery work is **undertaken** before dispatch. The orders are either full pallet loads for delivery to the bigger retailers or smaller orders from the ground level picking **bays** for the independent shops.

(adapted from: www.LogisticsHandling.com)

true (=T) or false (=F)

☐ 1. *Amethyst* has 600 full-time employees.

☐ 2. At peak periods less than 100 trailers a day arrive.

☐ 3. The contents of each trailer are put into stock before orders are picked.

☐ 4. The articulated forklift truck is perfectly suited to working in broader aisles.

☐ 5. Full pallets are delivered to certain aisles.

☐ 6. Once picked, the orders are dispatched immediately.

WORD BANK

aisle	Gang, Mittelgang
articulated forklift truck	Gelenk-Hubwagen
bay	Bucht, Laderaum
brand	Markenzeichen
contents	Inhalt
to dispatch	verschicken
to extract	entnehmen
narrow	eng, schmal
peak period	Spitzenzeit
stocktaking	Inventur
storage area	Lagerfläche
trailer	Container, Anhänger
to undertake	abwickeln, ausführen

4.1.7. WRITING

Find a subheading for each of the three paragraphs in the text "Toy Story" on page 64. Hide your three subheadings in a word field like the one on page 31. Make your neighbour find them.

4.1.8. MEDIATION

Your colleague doesn't understand English very well and asks you to summarise the "Toy Story". Read the text again and make notes of the important points. Then write a short summary in German.

4.2. Packing Goods

4.2.1. VOCABULARY

Match the types of packing to the pictures.

barrel | ~~bottle~~ | cardboard box | container | ~~pallet~~ | ~~sack~~

sack

barrel

bottle

container

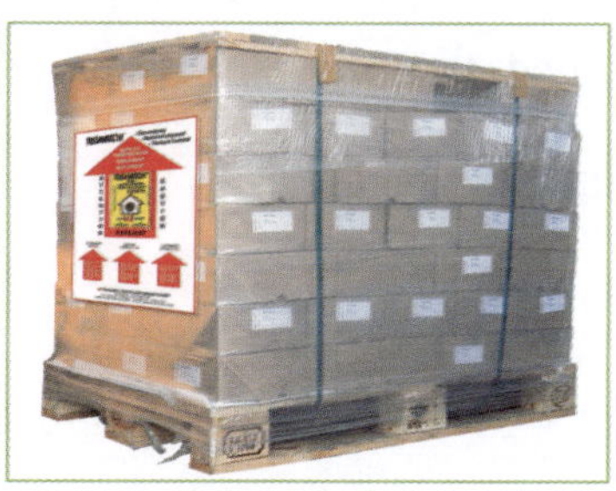

pallet

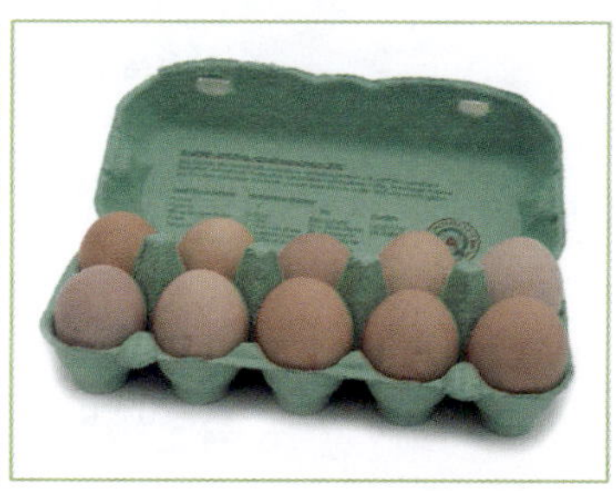

card board box

4.2.2. READING

Read the text and find the English equivalents of some highlighted terms.

Packaging

Packaging can be described as a coordinated system of preparing goods for transport, warehousing, logistics, **sale** and end use. Packaging contains, **protects**, **preserves**, informs, sells and makes transport safe.

Suitable packaging of a product is a critical factor in logistics. Without it, many logistics processes could not be performed at all or could be carried out only at great additional cost. The function of packaging is not just to protect the product from mechanical or climatic **stresses** during **delivery**. It affects many other jobs.

These include providing information about the contents as well as enabling and facilitating transport, handling, **storage** and order picking. Packaging can have features that add **convenience** in **distribution**, handling, **stacking**, display, sale, opening, reclosing, use, **dispensing** and **reuse**. The packaging and **labels** can be used by marketers to **encourage** potential buyers to **purchase** the product at the **point of sale**.

Etikett	labels	Verkauf	point of sale
schützen	protect	Lagerung	storage
Verbraucher-freundlichkeit	convenience	kaufen	purchase
konservieren	dispensing	Auslieferung	delivery

4.2.3. VOCABULARY

Find words in the text above which fit these definitions or explanations.

a. protects from mechanical stress	pachaging
b. transport goods from one place to another	
c. is inside the packaging	paching material
d. where goods are sold	point of sale
e. are used by marketers to encourage buyers	
f. the state of being useful, functional and advantageous	
g. cannot be performed without packaging	

4.2.4. READING

Read the text once more. Say whether the statements are true or false. Correct the false ones.

true (=T) or false (=F)

[ ] 1. Packaging is an uncoordinated system.

[ ] 2. Without packaging many logistics processes could be carried out at low costs.

[ ] 3. Packaging protects the product during delivery.

[ ] 4. Packaging enables storage.

[ ] 5. Packaging can be used by customers to sell the product.

4.2.5. MATCHING

Match the English words and phrases with the German equivalents.

[d]	1. adhesive tape	a. Füllmittel
[f]	2. bubble bag	b. zerbrechlich
[h]	3. corrugated board	c. Packmittel
[a]	5. filling material	d. Klebe-/Packband
[b]	6. fragile	e. vor Nässe schützen
[e]	7. to keep dry	f. Luftkissenpolster
i [scribbled]	8. package	g. Mehrwegpalette
[c]	9. packing material	h. Stapelbehälter
[j]	10. point of sale	i. Packstück
[g]	11. returnable pallet	j. Verkaufsplatz /-stelle
[h]	12. stackable bin	k. Wellpappe

4.2.6. DISCUSSION

Why is it important to have different types of packaging? Discuss in small groups. Make notes and present your results to the class. Use the vocabulary from exercise 4.2.5.

SKILLS

If you have to hold a presentation, the followings tips might be useful for you:

1. Inform yourself about the topic of the presentation carefully.
2. Think about the way you want to present your topic.
3. Make sure that the technical equipment is available and in good condition.
4. Only write notes and speak freely to the class.
5. Prepare yourself for questions and have further information at hand.
6. Try to keep eye contact with the class and the teacher.

4.2.7. MATCHING

Which type(s) of packing is (are) suitable for each good?

4.2.8. LISTENING FOR GIST

Listen to the interview with Julian Carroll and tell what it is about. Julian Carroll has been the Managing Director of the European Organisation for Packaging and the Environment *(EUROPEN)* since 1993.

4.2.9. LISTENING FOR DETAIL

Please answer the following questions after listening to the interview again.

a. What does Julian Carroll say about packing and sustainability?

b. How can environmental impacts of packaging be minimised?

c. How can packaging materials provide solutions according to Julian Carroll?

d. How can packaging materials play their part in reducing CO_2?

WORD BANK

convenience	Bequemlichkeit, Verbraucherfreundlichkeit
to dispense	entnehmen
distribution	Versand
to encourage	ermuntern
label	Etikett, Aufkleber
marketer	Vermarkter
point of sale	Kasse, Verkaufsplatz
to preserve sth.	etwas aufbewahren
to reuse	wiederverwenden
to sell	verkaufen
to stack	aufschichten, stapeln
stress	Belastung, Druck
storage	Einlagerung

4.2.10. WORKING WITH WORDS

Read the interview you have listened to and start a discussion about what Julian Carroll, former Managing Director of *EUROPEN*, is talking about packaging in the future.

Interviewer: **Everyone knows that in our throw-away society, waste and waste management have become an immense problem. And in times of globalisation goods travel long distances before they arrive at the end consumer. Both issues have an impact on your business. From your point of view, what is important in packaging? And what changes can we expect in the coming years regarding European and national standards?**

Julian Carroll: Good packaging reduces product waste and helps to centralise the **processing** and distribution of products. If we pack products well, we make sure that they arrive safely, clean and undamaged at their destination. By doing this, we help people across society to **maintain** acceptable living standards.

More attention has been paid to packaging recently, as it is becoming more and more important to find long-term solutions, that is so-called **sustainability**. I don't expect any new laws for packaging at European level, but there could be some at national level, simply because everyone is **confronted** with packaging in some way. We should do more to explain to policy makers, how **essential** the right packaging is and that it can support a society which wants to have long-term solutions. Correct packaging is a part of this solution, not its problem.

Interviewer: **Is there such a thing as "sustainable packaging"? Which principles need to be respected to ensure that the impacts of packaging on the environment are kept to a minimum?**

Julian Carroll: EUROPEN looks at the **entire life cycle** of a product and tries to adapt packaging to these needs. We do not believe in "sustainable packaging" as such, but want to help with our concepts to make the whole process of packing and delivering goods sustainable.
We think, for example, that the right material for packaging must be used. Steel is in a very good position here, because it is part of a responsible recycling system. By using the best type of packaging for each product, we can achieve improvements in three different fields: we can reduce the overall impact on the environment, we are able to find economic solutions and there is a clear **social benefit**.

Interviewer: **Food waste is an issue which is much discussed in European politics (or even in global politics). How do you think packaging materials can provide solutions?**

Julian Carroll: One of the basic concepts of packaging is to extend the **shelf life** of food in order to prevent the product going bad before it is consumed. Everything you can do to extend the shelf life of a product is a plus.
Another important point is that less organic waste is produced when food and beverages are packed in one place. When companies process food in larger amounts, many of the by-products that are produced are still worth something because of their quantity. At home, these things would be thrown away, because the amount is too small to do anything with them.
How important is packaging when it comes to the prevention of food waste? I would say very important. What we offer is a vision of how to make the whole process more sustainable by the right packaging.

Interviewer: **Everyone these days recognises the importance of reducing CO_2. How do you think packaging materials can play their part? How can steel contribute?**

Julian Carroll: CO_2 production stands for energy consumption, and energy is consumed when we manufacture packaging, transport goods and **dispose of** waste. For steel, the energy needed to recycle a steel **can** into a new steel product is a lot less than making new steel from **iron ore**. Modern steel containers are very light, and this also helps to reduce the amount of CO_2 which is produced in transportation. And lastly, of course, steel's recycling figures are the highest for any form of packaging. In 2008, 71 percent of steel packaging was recycled in Europe. This represents about 2.6 million tons of food and drinks cans and other steel containers, which were recycled and therefore saved four million of tons of CO_2. This is a very convincing argument.

(adapted from: Steel for Packaging Update. August 2010, Brussels)

4.2.11. GROUP WORK

Think about order picking and packaging in the future and present your ideas to the class. Use the following terms (translate first).

environment		sustainability	
energy		waste	
responsible		economic	

4.2.12. WRITING

Comment on the following statement by a marketer. Write 80 to 100 words.

"The main purpose of packaging is to sell the product and not to safe the environment."

WORD BANK

can	Dose
to confront sth.	etwas gegenüberstehen
consumption	Verbrauch
to contribute	beisteuern, einen Beitrag leisten
to dispose	entsorgen
essential	notwendig, grundlegend
iron ore	Eisenerz
life cycle	Lebensdauer
to maintain sth.	etwas aufrecht erhalten
processing	Bearbeitung, Verarbeitung
shelf life	Haltbarkeit
social benefit	gesellschaftlicher Nutzen
sustainability	Nachhaltigkeit, Zukunftsfähigkeit

HOW TO USE Word Order

Wortstellung in Aussagesätzen:
- normale Wortstellung:

Subjekt (wer)	Verb (macht)	Objekt (was)
I	pick	orders.
The teacher	speaks	English.

Wortstellung in Fragen:
- ist das Fragewort Subjekt, gilt die normale Worstellung:

Subjekt (wer)	Verb (macht)	Objekt (was)
Who	is reading	the book?

- in allen anderen Fällen wird ein Hilfsverb verwendet:

Objekt	Hilfsverb	Subjekt	Verb
What	did	you	see?

Achtung:

– in Nebensätzen bleibt diese Wortstellung immer erhalten	I always finish at five o'clock because **my train leaves the station** at half past five.
– Adverbien der Häufigkeit, die aus einem Wort bestehen, z. B. usually, sometimes etc., stehen vor dem (Voll-)Verb	I **always** pick the new orders.
– Adverbien der Häufigkeit, die aus mehreren Wörtern bestehen, z. B. this week, every day etc., stehen am Satzende	I unload the lorries **every morning.**

4.2.13. EXERCISE

a. Form sentences with the words below. Note the correct word order.

1. tea / drinks / my mother / every afternoon

My mother drinks tea every afternoon

2. not / English / understand / he / can

He can not understand English

3. brought / me / the postman / a letter

The postman brought me a letter

4. broke / the glasses / who

Who broke the glasses?

5. where / bought / this book / have / you

Where have you bought this book?

6. he / why / did / late / come

why did he come late?

7. the train / here / come

Here comes the train

8. work / at seven o'clock / I / in the morning / start

I start working at seven o'clock

9. over the fence / into the garden / the cat / jumped

The cat jumped over the fence into the garden

10. Jeremy / a kiss / yesterday / Helen / gave

Helen gave Jeremy a kiss yesterday

b. Form questions out of sentences 7 to 10 in exercise a.

7. the train / here / come

When does the train come?

8. work / at seven o'clock / I / in the morning / start

When do you start working?

9. over the fence / into the garden / the cat / jumped

How got the cat into the garden?

10. Jeremy / a kiss / yesterday / Helen / gave

Who gave who a kiss yesterday?

HOW TO USE

Adjectives and Adverbs

Anwendung:	
Adjektive beschreiben das Substantiv näher. Sie stehen entweder vor dem Substantiv oder nach dem Verb „to be".	I like **interesting** work. My work is **interesting**.
Adverbien beschreiben, wie jemand etwas tut oder wie etwas geschieht. Sie bestimmen Verben, Adjektive oder andere Adverbien näher.	He drives the forklift **carefully**. (Bezug auf das Verb) Ronald is **extremely** clever in picking goods. (Bezug auf das Adjektiv) Diana learns warning signs **extremely** quickly. (Bezug auf das Adverb)
Bildung von Adverbien: Adverb = Adjektiv + „-ly" **Achtung:** – endet das Adjektiv auf „y", verwandelt sich dieses in ein „i", z.B. happy – happily, easy – easily – einige Adverbien haben die gleiche Form wie das Adjektiv, z.B. hard – hard, late – late, fast – fast – einige Wörter sehen aus wie Adverbien, haben aber eine andere Bedeutung, z.B. hardly (kaum), lately (kürzlich, neulich)	

4.2.14. WRITING

Fill in the correct form of the adjective or adverb.

He is a very (1) reliable (reliable) worker.

The secretary works on the computer (2) efficiently (efficient).

I should learn my vocabulary more (3) precisely (precise).

We have (4) regularly (regular) meetings with all the team members.

I was able to buy this machine quite (5) cheap (cheap).

Yesterday, we had a very (6) funny (funny) situation at work.

My teacher was very (7) angry (angry) with me because I had forgotten my homework.

He shouted at me (8) angrily (angry).

My new job is very (9) interesting (interesting).

I looked at the new girl in my class (10) curiously (curious).

4.2.15. EXERCISE

Describe your job, your workplace and your working environment in five sentences with adjectives.

Example: *I work at a big warehouse.*

1. ______________________________

2. ______________________________

3. ______________________________

4. ______________________________

5. ______________________________

4.2.16. EXERCISE

Describe how your boss and your colleagues do things using five adverbs.

Example: *My colleague Peter drives the forklift recklessly.*

1. ______________________________

2. ______________________________

3. ______________________________

4. ______________________________

5. ______________________________

4.3. Business Correspondence – Orders

4.3.1. MATCHING

Study the chart of the Incoterms 2010. Then complete the tables below using the words in the box.

INCOTERMS 2010

The INCOTERMS (international commercial terms) are determined by the International Chamber of Commerce. They help facilitate understanding delivery terms in international trade. The INCOTERMS 2010 are the revised form of Incoterms 2000 and came into force on 1 January 2011. They contain the following set of terms:

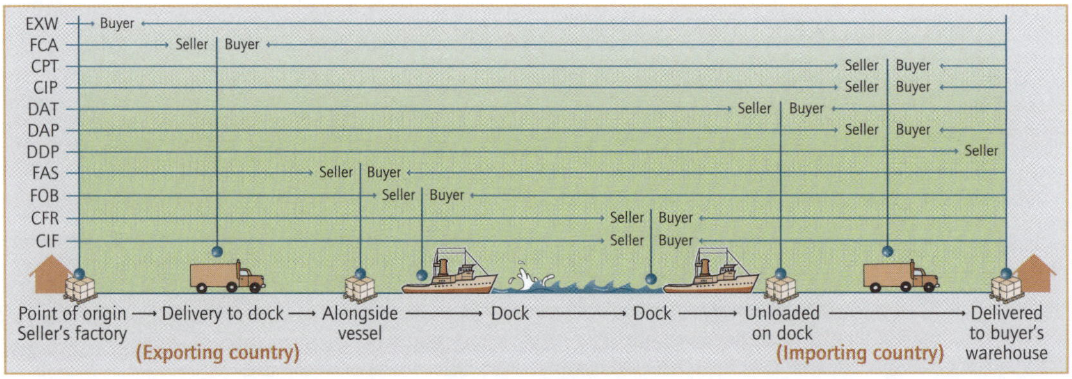

ab Werk | carriage and insurance paid to | cost, insurance and freight | CPT | DAT | delivered duty paid | FOB | free carrier | frei Längsseite Schiff | Kosten und Fracht

Incoterms 2010 applicable for all modes of transport

EXW	ex works	named place	
FCA		named place	frei Frachtführer
	carriage paid to	named place of destination	frachtfrei
CIP		named place of destination	frachtfrei, versichert
	delivered at terminal	named place	geliefert Terminal
DAP	delivered at place	named place	geliefert benannter Ort
DDP		named place of destination	geliefert verzollt

Incoterms 2010 only applicable for sea and inland waterway transport

FAS	free alongside ship	named port of shipment	
	free on board	named port of shipment	frei an Bord
CFR	cost and freight	named port of destination	
CIP		named port of destination	Kosten, Versicherung u. Fracht

4.3.2. READING

Read the text and decide on the right word in the shaded fields.

Orders are replies to/for formal offers. They are often placed by sending a letter, e-mail or fax to/at the supplier. Many companies use a preprinted order or purchase order form which/who contains blank spaces. This form has to be filled in/up by the buyer giving the required details an order should contain. Nevertheless, it is still common practise to order goods with/by sending a letter, fax or e-mail. Regarding faxes, there is no specific form or layout. The companies may design their individual layout for/about fax transmissions.

4.3.3. ANALYSING

Put the jumbled parts of the following order by fax into the right order. Use the numbers 1 to 10.

20-OCT-20..   14:43 PM   010789650   1/1

SHAMROCK & HARPER LOGISTICS
Kingswood Business Park – Dublin 22
Phone: 010789654   Fax: 010789650   E-mail: shamrock@s&h.ie

To: Tom Branson
Harkley Lifting Ltd.
From: Flore Kenmoe
Date: 20 October 20..
Subject: Order No. 1456
Pages: 1

We look forward to receiving your confirmation of this order soon.

Many thanks for your offer of 6 September 20.. .

As we are in urgent need of the ordered items, we would appreciate delivery by 15 November at the latest.

Quantity	Item No.	Description	Unit price	Total
10	3310	Heavy Duty Ratchet Strap	€ 11.50	€ 115.00
15	6610	Auto Ratchet Strap 1,8 mtr.	€ 12.00	€ 180.00
20	6680	Auto Rachet Strap 3 mtr.	€ 14.00	€ 140.00

Prices are quoted free domicile, exclusive of VAT, payable at 30 days net, 14 days 2%.

Yours sincerely
Flore Kenmoe
Flore Kenmoe
Purchasing

We have studied your quotation and found the offered ratchet straps satisfactory. Therefore, we take pleasure in ordering as follows:

Dear Mr Branson

4.3.4. ANALYSING

You work for *ABC Storage Ltd.* 21/24 Broom Road, Bristol BS4 5RG. The company wants to expand the storage capacity of its warehouse.
Study the quotation from *Bakker Plast BV* and your forwarding agent's pricelist. Use the calculation form below to find out the most favourable price. Then order 200 pallet boxes of item no. 40-10202.

From: bakker@plast.nl
To: morton@abc.co.uk
Date: 10 October 20__
Subject: Enquiry for pallet boxes

Dear Mr Morton

Quotation No. 7802/jh

Thank you very much for your message and your interest in our pallets.

We would now like to submit the following quotation:

Item no. 40-10202 - Plastic Pallet Box L 202
Dimension 1200x1000x750 mm - volume 616 litres - max load per box 450 kg
EXW £225.00
FOB Rotterdam £265.00
CIF Southampton £305.00

Prices are to be understood inclusive of VAT.
On orders over 150 units we can grant a 10% quantity discount.
Terms of payment: 30 days net, 10 days 2%.
Delivery can be effected within 10 days from receipt of order.

We look forward to welcoming you as a new customer.

Yours sincerely
Jan Holst
Bakker-Plast BV * Sontplein 10 * 9723 BZ Groningen
Phone: 0031(0)6689-124589 * Fax: 0031(0)6689-124580

McPherson
Transport and Haulage

PRICELIST

Sea carriage	£45
Road transport Southampton – Bristol	£15
Road transport Groningen – Rotterdam	£25

CALCULATION FORM

Delivery Term	Price Bakker Plast	Road Groningen-Rotterdam	Sea carriage	Road Southhampton-Bristol	Total
EXW	£225	£25	£45	£15	£310
FOB					
CIF					

4.3.5. WRITING

Use the order form and place the order according to your price calculation in ex. 4.3.4.

PURCHASE ORDER FORM

⇨ Fax 0031(0)6689 - 124589 ⇨ Phone 0031(0)6689 - 124580

Bakker – Plast B.V., Sontplein 10, 9723 BZ Groningen

Sender/invoice recipient

Order No.: ________. as per quotation No.__________

Code No.	Item	QTY	Unit price £	Total £
		Subtotal		
		Less discount 10%		
		Grand Total £		

Please select your mode of transport

EXW ☐ FOB Rotterdamm ☐ CIF Southampton ☐

Signature: ______________ Date: ____________________

WORD BANK

to be affected	beeinflusst werden
confirmation	Bestätigung
free domicile	frei Haus
quotation	Preisangebot
recipient	Abnehmer, Empfänger
storage capacity	Lagerkapazität

4.3.6. CROSSWORD

Fill in the English translation of the words below.

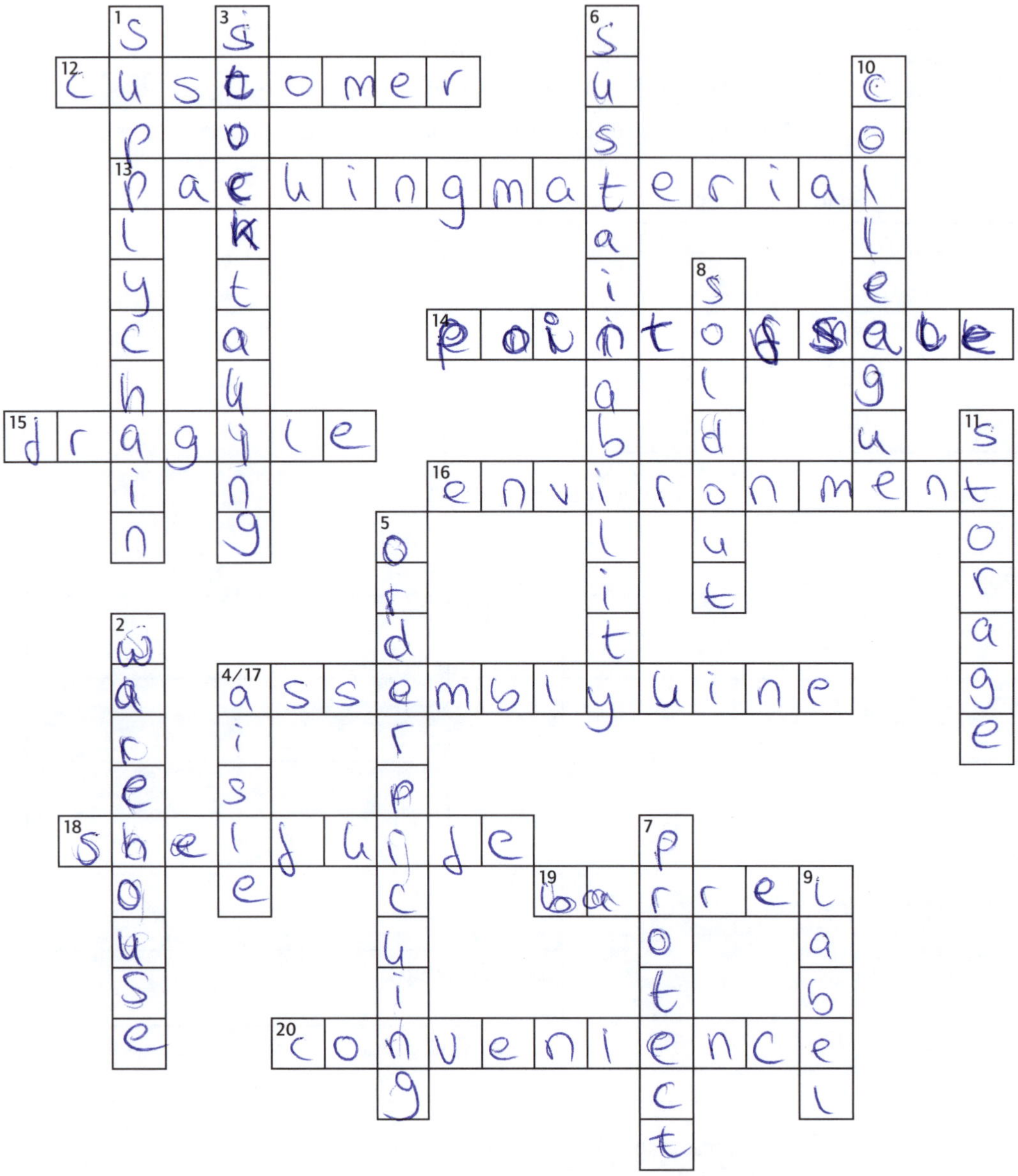

DOWN

1. Lieferkette
2. Lagerhalle
3. Inventur
4. Gang
5. kommissionieren
6. Nachhaltigkeit
7. schützen
8. ausverkauft
9. Etikett
10. Kollege/Kollegin
11. Einlagerung

ACROSS

12. Kunde
13. Packmittel
14. Verkaufsplatz
15. zerbrechlich
16. Umwelt
17. Fließband
18. Haltbarkeit
19. Fass
20. Verbraucherfreundlichkeit

5 Transport and Logistics

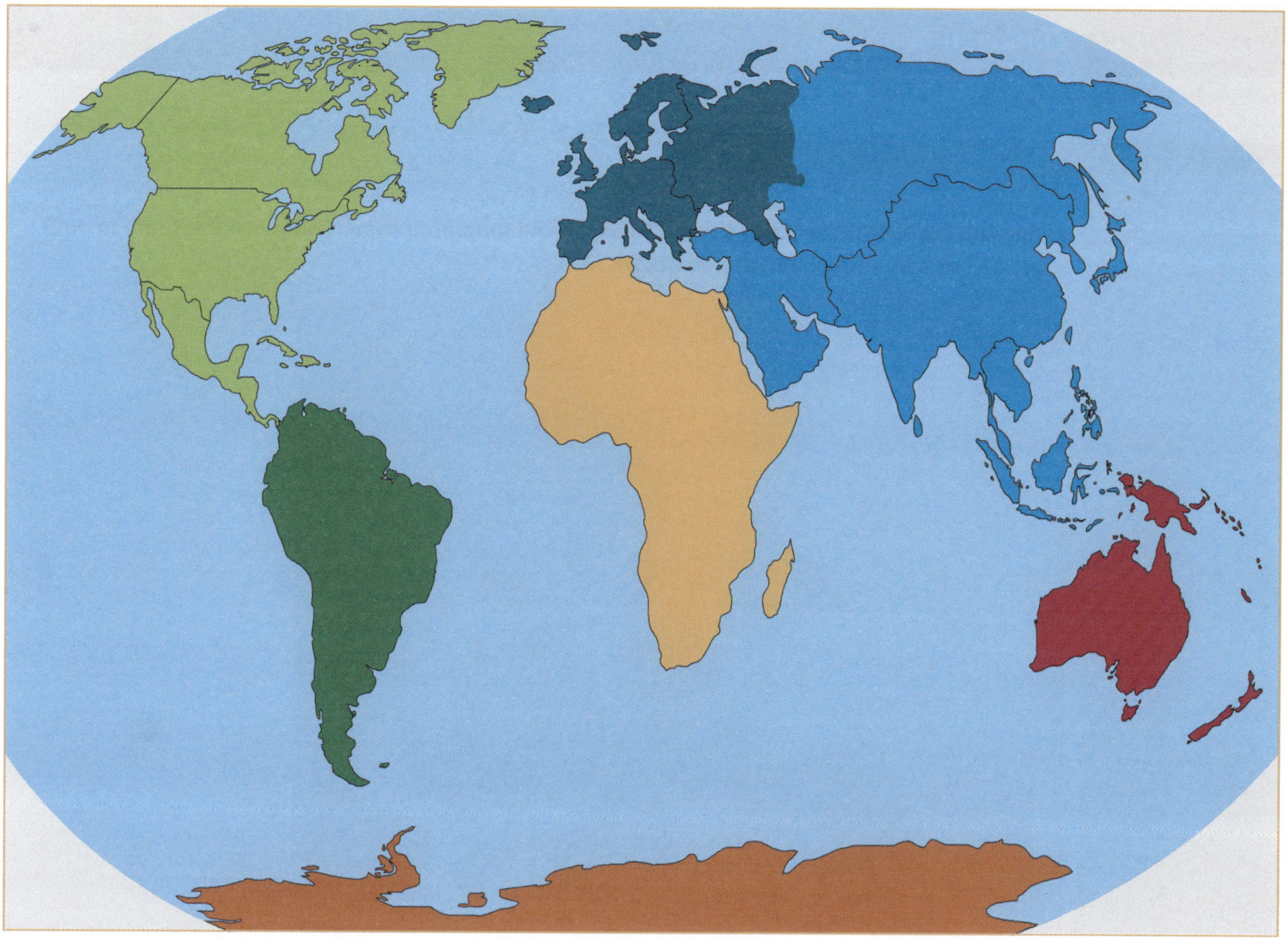

ANALYSING

Mark on the world map:

- the seven most commonly recognized continents
- the five oceans: Pacific Ocean, Atlantic Ocean, Indian Ocean, Antarctic Ocean, Arctic Ocean. Use the letters a to e.
- the world's five largest economies in terms of the GDP (Gross Domestic Product)
- countries you do business with (customers or suppliers)

SKILLS

Capitalisation in written English

In order to avoid unnecessary mistakes, obey these three capitalisation rules:

1. We capitalise the first letter at the beginning of a new sentence.
2. The pronoun 'I' is always capitalised.
3. Proper names are capitalised, e. g.:
   - personal names (Elisabeth)
   - names of companies, institutions, brands etc. (Deutscher Bundestag)
   - names of cities, countries, continents and geographical terms (London, Spain, Africa, The River Elbe)
   - months, days of the week, bank holidays (June, Saturday, Christmas)

5

5.1. European Countries

5.1.1. MATCHING

Name the European countries from 1 to 31 on the map of Europe. Complete the table in your exercise book by using the scheme below.

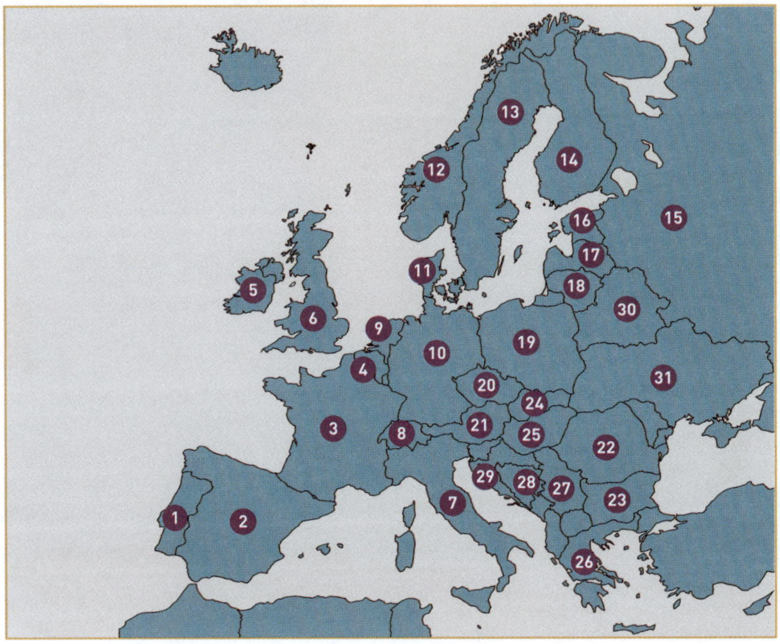

	Country	Capital	Language	Currency
1				
2				
...				

5.2. Organising a Transport

5.2.1. BRAINSTORMING

Your colleague Paul, who is normally in charge of planning routes for the international trade, has become seriously ill. Your manager wants you to organise a transport from Hamburg to Hong Kong in China. What do you have to keep in mind if you want to make the transport a success? Use a mind map for collecting your ideas.

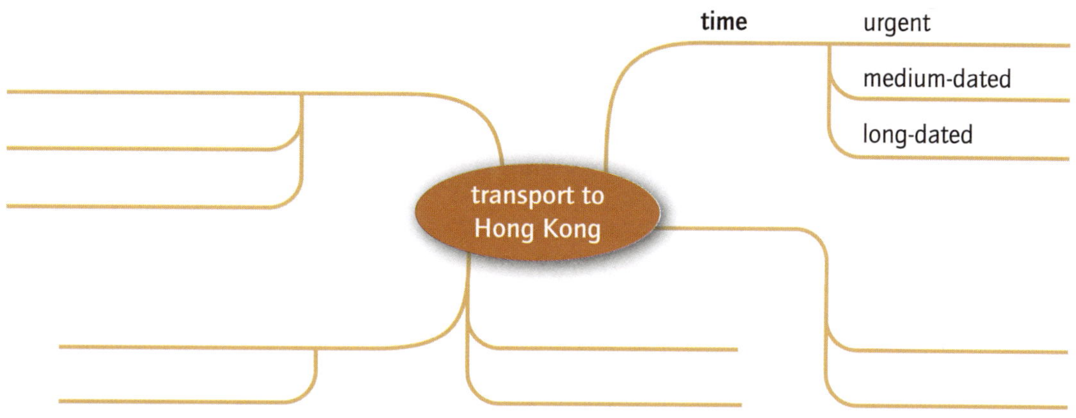

5.2.2. READING

Read the e-mail from Paul Smith and complete the text with words from the box.

condition | costs | customer | mode of transport | route | screws | urgently | warehouse

Von:	paul.smith@yahoo.com
An:	
Datum:	
Betreff:	

Hi Sarah,

In general, organising a transport requires a lot of individual knowledge and a whole bunch of aspects that have to be taken into consideration. Your job is to bring the customer needs and your internal **workflow** together.

Before the goods leave the (1) warehouse towards China, a couple of questions have to be answered: When do you have to send the **consignment** so that the (2) customer gets it on time? It is rather obvious that this information is needed in order to decide which (3) mode of transport you have to choose.

Imagine your client needs the goods (4) urgently and you decide to send it by ship! That leads you to another important question: Which mode of transport **fits** best for the goods you are going to transport? I am sure you agree that there is a difference whether you just send a packet of (5) screws, a **pallet** packed with **fragile** glass or 200 tons of **bulk cargo**. Moreover, you should also think about how to pack your goods so that they arrive at the buyer's **premises** in perfect (6) condition. The decision on appropriate packing material is closely related to safety aspects. Ignoring that can **cause** much trouble and additional (7) costs for the **sender**.

Finally, whenever you plan a (8) route and the right mode of transport, you need to think about what (environmental) costs are involved when sending goods. All right, I do hope I could help you!

Best regards
Paul

5.2.3. MATCHING

a. See whether the contents of the e-mail correspond in any way with your ideas in your mind map. Compile a list with the major issues you have to bear in mind.
b. Match the highlighted terms in the text with the German equivalents in the box.

Arbeitsablauf | Lieferung | Palette | passen | Räumlichkeit | Schüttgut | Versender | verursachen | zerbrechlich

a.	*workflow*	
b.		
c.		
d.		
e.		
f.		
g.		
h.		
i.		

5.3. Going Global

5.3.1. SURVEY

a. Read the following quotations of warehouse logistics operators. Which one do you most agree with?
b. Work in small groups. Create questions for a questionnaire and present it to the class.
c. Ask three to five colleagues and report to the class next week.

"People say globalisation is bad for the jobs in Germany because many companies shift their production to low-wage countries."

"I do not care about globalisation. Our company is too small as becoming part in the global trade."

"Globalisation has turned the world into a huge toy shop with everyone of us as potential seller and buyer."

"20 years ago we did business nationwide or with companies in Austria, Swiss, Belgium or the Netherlands. Nowadays, we receive containers from China, consignments from Brazil or India and we send off goods to Korea."

5.3.2. READING

Read the article and number the paragraphs in the correct order 1 to 5. Then answer the questions below.

The Features of Globalisation

☐ No technology has had such a huge impact on the globalisation as the Internet. It **spans** the world and makes it easy to communicate and to do business. **Literally**, every one can **set up** a business and buy and sell via the Internet.

☐ In conclusion, whether we want it or not, globalisation greatly affects our lives. You decide whether you buy a computer mouse for little more than two euros including shipping or strawberries at wintertime.

☐ But there are also many negative aspects of globalisation such as the **exploitation** of poor countries and **interdependence**. That means countries **depend on** each other in terms of import and export. Political or economic crises might lead to a **shortage** of goods. Additionally, companies move their production **abroad** or outsource departments. Very often many people lose their jobs.

☐ Over the decades, the global trade amongst the economies has increased enormously. Globalisation in the modern sense is characterised by cheap production and shipping. Multinational companies produce and sell worldwide and have **gained** a huge market power.

☐ Globalisation, often described as phenomenon of the 21st century, has its **origins** in the fifteenth century as European merchants started to discover the world and to sell and buy worldwide.

1. **Which features of globalisation are mentioned?**

____

2. **What are negative aspects of globalisation?**

____

WORD BANK

abroad	Ausland, ins Ausland
to depend on	abhängig sein von
exploitation	Ausbeutung, Ausnutzung
extent	Ausmaß, Umfang
feature	Merkmal
Gross Domestic Product (GDP)	Bruttoinlandsprodukt
interdependence	Abhängigkeit, Wechselbeziehung
literally	wortwörtlich
origin	Ursprung
to outsource	ausgliedern
questionnaire	Fragebogen
to set up	arrangieren
to shift	verlagern
shortage	Mangel
to span	umfassen, umspannen

5.3.3. DISCUSSION

Work in pairs. Discuss one of the negative aspects in 5.3.2 and add further issues.

5.3.4. WRITING

Comment on one of the quotations on page 84, using your own knowledge and ideas.

SKILLS

How to write a discussion
1. Start with a general introduction on the topic and say whether you agree or disagree with the statement.
2. Collect and group your ideas which speak for and against the statement.
3. Make a concluding statement in which you sum up your arguments.

HOW TO USE

Comparison of Adjectives

Anwendung:	
Adjektive beschreiben Eigenschaften, z. B. fast (schnell). Mit Hilfe der Steigerung von Adjektiven, z. B. faster (schneller = Komparativ), the fastest (das schnellste = Superlativ), wird ausgedrückt, in welchem Ausmaß eine Eigenschaft vorhanden ist.	A bike is quite **fast**. A car is **faster** than a bike. A train is the **fastest** vehicle.
Bildung: Komparativ = Adjektiv + „-er" Superlativ = Adjektiv + „-est"	
Vergleich, Möglichkeit 1: „… -er / more … than …"	The plane is **faster than** the train.
Vergleich, Möglichkeit 2: „… (not) as … as …"	The transport by train is **not as** expensive **as** by plane.

Achtung:
- endet das Adjektiv auf „e", entfällt dieses bei der Steigerung, z. B. large – larg**er** – larg**est**
- endet das Adjektiv auf „y", verwandelt sich dieses in ein „i", z. B. busy – bus**ier** – bus**iest**
- nach einem kurzen Vokal wird ein Konsonant am Ende des Verbs verdoppelt, z. B. big – bigg**er** – bigg**est**
- ist das Adjektiv zweisilbig und endet auf –y, -ow, -er oder –le, wird es wie ein einsilbiges Adjektiv gesteigert, z. B. happy – happ**ier** – happ**iest**, narrow – narrow**er** – narrow**est**, clever – clever**er** – clever**est**, gentle – gentl**er** – gentl**est**
- zweisilbige Adjektive, die auf der ersten Silbe betont werden, sowie drei- und mehrsilbige Adjektive und Partizipien werden mit **„more"** und **„most"** bzw. **„less"** und **„least"** gesteigert, z. B. expensive – more expensive – most expensive / less expensive – least expensive
- Steigerung von good: better – best, Steigerung von bad: worse – worst

5.3.5. EXERCISE

Fill in the correct form of the words in brackets (comparative or superlative).

1. Our warehouse is (1) *bigger* (big) than yours.
2. This road is even (2) *narrower* (narrow) and (3) *dirtier* (dirty) than the last one.
3. English is one of the (4) *easiest* (easy) languages and Chinese probably the (5) *most difficult* (difficult) language.
4. My colleagues speak English (6) *better* (good) than me.
5. It was the (7) *worst* (bad) day in my life.

5.4. Modes of Transport

5.4.1. DISCUSSION

Besides human-powered transportation such as riding a bicycle or watercraft rowing and animal-powered transportation such as the transport by horses, donkeys, camels or elephants, the 21st century logistics is characterised by highly technologised modes of transportation. Describe the drawing below. Identify the four modes of transport and explain the most common means of transport. Use the grid below.

	Modes of transport			
	by road	by rail	by sea	by air
Means of transport				

5.4.2. LISTENING FOR GIST

Michael Meier works as a warehouse logistics operator for *Logistik-Weltweit GmbH* in Hamburg, Germany. His company supplies storage technology and services to wholesalers all over Europe. First read through the following statements, then listen to the audio and decide whether the statements are true or false. If they are wrong correct them.

true (=T) or false (=F)

☐ 1. Michael has spoken to Pauline before.

☐ 2. Pauline wants to speak with Michael about the latest delivery of electronic control units.

☐ 3. Three of the ten devices of the last delivery were damaged, five were sold and two are still on stock.

☐ 4. Pauline's customer needs the device urgently.

☐ 5. *Logistik-Weltweit GmbH* normally sends its goods by rail.

☐ 6. The transport by air is the fastest mode of transport.

☐ 7. Courier services are less reliable than transport by air.

☐ 8. They choose transport by road.

5.4.3. LISTENING FOR DETAIL

First read through the following sentences in which some words or phrases are missing. Next listen to the recording again and fill in the boxes.

Pauline: Good morning. My name is Pauline Bernard from *Atlor* in Calais. I would like to speak to Michael Meier, please.

Michael: (1) ________________. Who am I speaking to?

Pauline: This is Pauline Bernard from Atlor.

Michael: Oh, Pauline, nice to speak to you again! (2) ________________?

Pauline: Very well, thank you, and you?

Michael: I am fine, thank you. What can I do for you?

Pauline: Michael, we have got a serious problem. One of our biggest (3) ________________ needs an electronic control unit for an automated guided vehicle.

It is very (4) ________________ and he keeps on asking when we can (5) ________________.

Michael: I understand, Pauline. Did you not receive our last (6) ________________ with ten of the electronic control units you need now?

Pauline: Yes, we did, but all those units were sold within four days.
Michael: Hmm, so how do we get the devices from Hamburg to Calais (7) ________________ ?
We normally transport the goods by ship, but I suppose that will take much too long.
Pauline: Exactly. Time is getting short. We do need an alternative.
Michael: What about using the train?
Pauline: Possibly. It is even (8) ________________ than a ship but the transport time is 24 hours. We can't keep the customer waiting that long.
Michael: What do you think about sending the devices by air? It is the (9) ________________ mode of transport and you will get the delivery (10) ________________ .
Pauline: I agree with you, but what about the cost? I am sure (11) ________________ is less expensive and as (12) ________________ as by plane.
Michael: Listen. First, let me check the prices for the plane and for a courier service. I'll call you back (13) ________________ I have more information.
Pauline: Thank you Michael. Speak to you soon.
Michael: Bye, Pauline.

5.4.4. PRESENTATION

Work in small groups. Choose one mode of transport and discuss its advantages and disadvantages. Next present your results to the class. Each member of the group should prepare a 60-second talk.

5.4.5. ANALYSING

Form sentences in which you compare the different modes of transport. Use the data about the CO_2 emissions and the costs, and the words in the box.

Example: *Transport by rail is cheaper than by road.*

cheap | dangerous | economical | environmentally friendly | environmentally (un)friendly | expensive | fast | flexible | quick | reliable | risky | safe | secure | slow | time-consuming

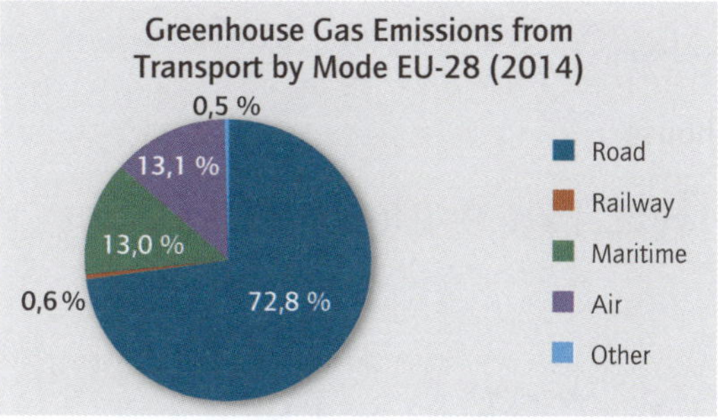

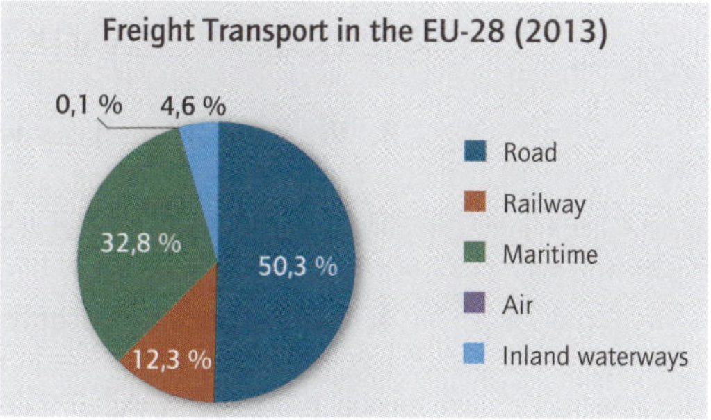

HOW TO USE **Passive Voice**

Anwendung:	
Aktiv: Verb im Aktiv drückt aus, was ein Subjekt macht.	Dinah **drives** the forklift. (Dinah fährt den Gabelstapler.)
Passiv: Verb im Passiv drückt aus, was mit dem Subjekt geschieht.	The forklift **is driven** by Dinah. (Der Gabelstapler wird von Dinah gefahren.)

Bildung:
Passive Voice = Form von „to be" + past participle („-ed" oder 3. Form des unregelmäßigen Verbs)

Zeit	**Aktiv**	**Passiv**
Simple Present	John packs parcels every day. (John packt jeden Tag Pakete.)	Parcels **are** pack**ed** by John every day. (Jeden Tag werden von John Pakete gepackt.)
Simple Past	John packed a parcel. (John packte ein Paket.)	A parcel **was** pack**ed** by John. (Ein Paket wurde von John gepackt.)
Present Continuous	John is packing a parcel. (John packt gerade ein Paket.)	A parcel **is being** pack**ed** by John. (Ein Paket wird gerade von John gepackt.)
Present Perfect	John has packed a parcel. (John hat ein Paket gepackt.)	A parcel **has been** pack**ed** by John. (Ein Paket wurde von John gepackt.)
Will-Future	John will pack a parcel. (John wird ein Paket packen.)	A parcel **will be** pack**ed** by John. (Ein Paket wird von John gepackt werden.)

Achtung:
- Bei der Umwandlung von Aktiv/Passiv darf die Zeit nicht gewechselt werden.

5.4.6. EXERCISE

Rewrite the sentences in passive voice.

1. Eric drives a forklift truck.

the forklift truck is driven by Eric.

2. Lucas sent of the consignment.

the consignment was sent by Lucas

3. We have cleaned our warehouse.

Our warehouse has been cleaned by us.

4. I will phone a customer.

A customer will be phoned by me.

5.4.8. READING

Read the text and answer the questions below.

Multimodal Transport

Over the past **decade** the world has seen a movement towards globalisation and trade liberalisation. In this process, national borders are increasingly disappearing and **trade barriers** have been reduced or do not exist anymore. This development requires changes in the type and quality of transport and logistics services and infrastructure. The massive growth in **containerisation** has shifted the modern transport from „port-to-port“ to „door-to-door“. Moreover, many companies have changed their production methods to be able to use containers for export and to **take advantage** of Multimodal Transport (MT).

MT, also called 'combined transport', can be defined as the chain that links different modes of transport into one complete process. The intelligent combination of transport by air, by road, by rail, or by sea ensures an efficient and cost-effective door-to-door movement of goods. Multimodal transports are **performed** under the responsibility of a single **transport operator**, known as a Multimodal Transport Operator (MTO), on one transport document.

In today's dynamic markets companies must be flexible to respond rapidly to **competition** and market changes. The **ultimate goal** is to "deliver greater value to customers or create more value at lower costs". Multimodal Transport is one option for companies to reduce costs and to improve customer service.

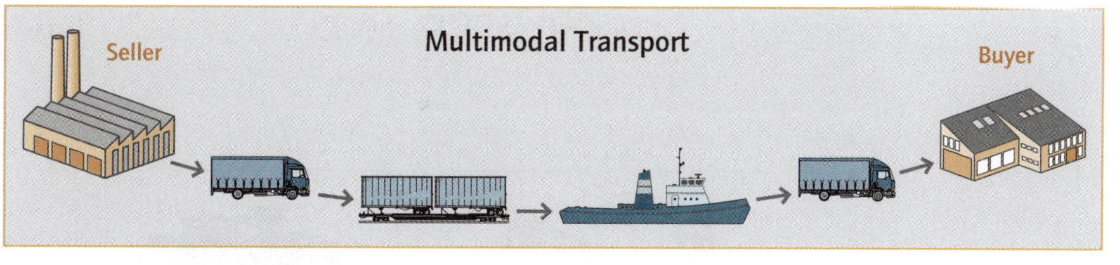

1. What is a Multimodal Transport?

2. Which advantages of MT are mentioned in the text?

WORD BANK

containerisation	Container-Transport
corporate image	Firmenbild
decade	Jahrzehnt
to perform	auftreten, durchführen
revenue	Umsatz
to take advantage of	einen Vorteil aus etwas ziehen
trade barrier	Handelsschranke
transport operator	Transportunternehmer
ultimate goal	Endziel

5.5. Material Handling Equipment for Internal Transport

5.5.1. MATCHING

Nowadays, most work processes in a warehouse are based on high-tech equipment. The photos show different material handling equipment that can be used depending on the size, weight and nature of the goods. Match the names below to the photos and find the German equivalence.

automated guided vehicle | forklift truck | electric stacker truck | reach truck | low-lift pallet truck | electric tow truck | hand pallet truck | high rack stacker

high rack stacker	automated guided vehicle	low-lift pallet truck	forklift truck

hand-pallet truck	reach truck	electric tow truck	electric stacker truck

5.5.2. ANALYSING

a. **Analyse the illustration on page 93 and mark the zones (1) – (6) on the storage plan.**
b. **In which zones is the material handling equipment pictured in 5.5.1 normally used?**
c. **Which other material handling equipment do you use in your daily work?**

(1) loading area with ramp	(3) shelf-storage system	(5) packing station
(2) receipt of goods	(4) order picking	(6) dispatch

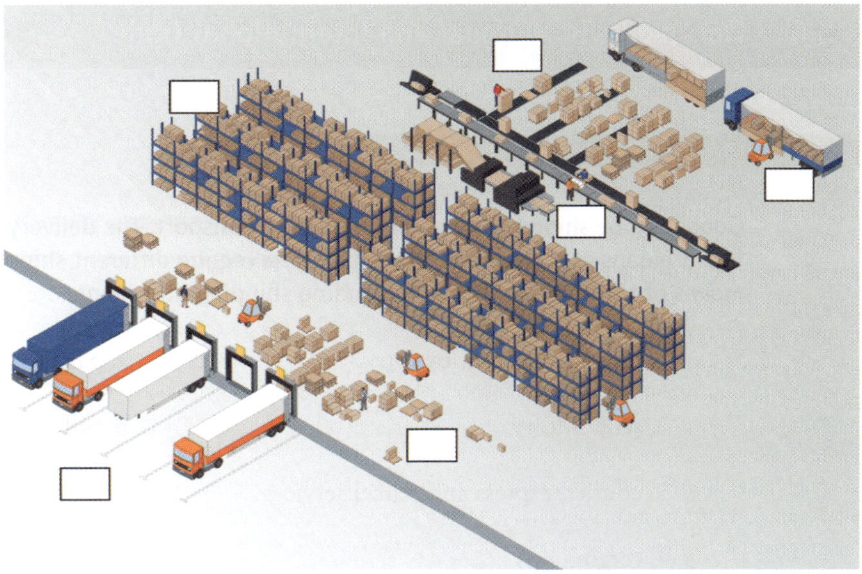

5.5.3. CREATIVE ACTIVITY

Draw a storage plan of your stock room. Then explain the different zones and their functions in the whole process. Use the words from 5.5.2.

5.5.4. MATCHING

Forklift trucks have become the most important material handling vehicle in modern warehouses. They are extensively used in warehouses for loading and off-loading.

Look at the parts of a forklift truck. Use the words in the box to complete the drawing.

counterbalance | driver's seat | engine compartment | fork | forklift fork | frame | lifting chain | lifting cylinder | mast | overhead guard | safety guard | tilt cylinders

(1) overhead guard

(2)

(3) driver's seat

(4) counterbalance

(5) tilt cylinders

(6) engine compartment

(7) frame

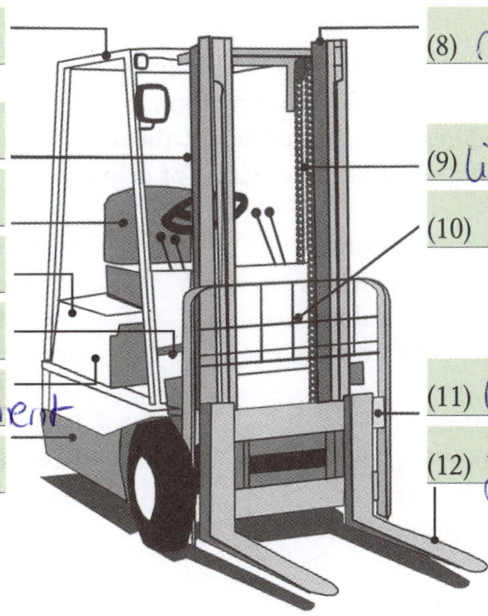

(8) mast

(9) lifting chain

(10) safety guard

(11) lifting cylinders

(12) forklift fork

5.6. Documents in National and International Trade

5.6.1. MATCHING

Goods can be shipped by the four modes of transport. The delivery can be performed by different means of transport. Different carriers require different shipping documents. Match the means of transport to the corresponding shipping documents.

☐	1. freight forwarder by lorry	a. parcel label
☐	2. seller's lorry	b. bill of lading
☐	3. courier, express and parcel services	c. air bill of lading
☐	4. cargo train	d. delivery note
☐	5. inland waterway vessel	e. consignment note/delivery note
☐	6. seagoing vessel	f. railway bill of lading
☐	7. transport plane	g. bill of lading

5.6.2. READING

a. **Read the text below carefully and fill in the commercial invoice on page 95. This is the invoice for the 200 pallet boxes of item no. 40-10202 you have ordered with the form on page 79.**

Delivery Notes

A delivery note is a document that **accompanies** a shipment of goods. It includes information about quantity, description, **grade**, weight and the delivery date of the goods delivered. The delivery note is issued by the supplier and a copy of the delivery note, signed by the buyer, is returned to the seller. It **serves** as a **proof** that the goods have been delivered. On delivery the buyer needs to check the note carefully. In case of damages the delivery can be **rejected**.

The **commercial invoice** sometimes serving as a delivery note is also issued by the supplier. In addition to the listed information, a commercial invoice also includes elements such as name and address of seller and buyer, the invoice number, unit price and total price, shipping details (number of packages) or terms of delivery and payment.

WORD BANK

to accompany	begleiten, beifügen
bill of lading	Frachtbrief
commercial invoice	Warenrechnung
freight forwarder	Spediteur
grade	Grad, Anspruchsklasse
parcel label	Paketaufkleber
proof	Beweis, Abzug
to reject	abweisen, ablehnen
seagoing vessel	Seeschiff
to serve	dienen, nützen

b. Discuss with your partner which difficulties might appear in filling in and checking delivery notes.

GT Global Transport Ltd.

Commercial invoice

Exporter/Shipper (name and adress)

Invoice number

Invoice date

Consignee

Manufacturing country

Terms of payment

Destination country

Freight

Other remarks

Item	Weight	Description of goods	Quantity	Unit price	Amount
Total weight			**Total quantity**	**Total invoice amount**	

Name of Shipper

Signature of Shipper

5.7. Business Correspondence – Complaints and Apologies

5.7.1. BRAINSTORMING

Read the text and with a partner brainstorm reasons for a complaint. Make a mind map from your results.

Sometimes Things Go Wrong

When selling products or services, mistakes sometimes happen. In this case the customer will complain to the supplier. Dealing with customer complaints is one of the most delicate issues in business as the aim is to satisfy and retain the customer. You should therefore respond to a complaint in a polite tone. Give the customer the feeling that you understand his/her problem and that you will solve the problem. The customer also expects you to take action either in granting a compensation or, if the complaint is not fully grounded, in suggesting a compromise. It should in any case meet the customer's expectations.

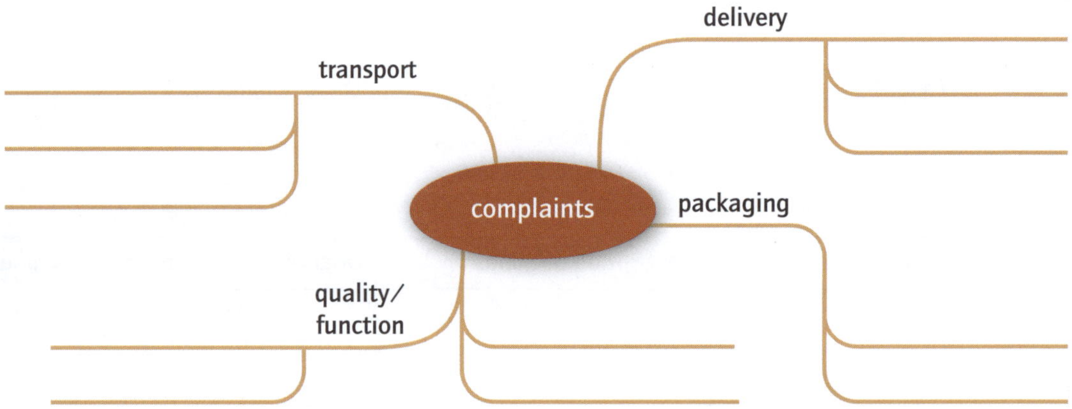

5.7.2. READING

Read the letter of complaint on page 97 and decide if the statements below are true or false.

true (=T) or false (=F)

t 1. The *FragranceMakers* received a consignment of bottles and jars.

f 2. 24 bottles are broken and 3 jars are missing.

t 3. They are sending photos of the bottles and jars to prove the damage.

t 4. The damage was caused by rough handling in transit.

f 5. The *FragranceMakers* do not need the replacement before next month.

f 6. The damaged items are returned to the supplier.

From:	bruce.haven@fragrancemakers.com
To:	lex.cole@fancybottles.co.uk
Date:	10 October 20__
Subject:	Damaged items

Dear Mr Cole

Our order no. 1234
Your packing list no. 6543

We are writing with reference to the above mentioned consignment of perfume bottles and jars we received yesterday.

On unpacking the items we found that 9 of the 24 bottles in parcel no. 5 were completely broken and 3 of the 30 jars in parcel no. 6 were badly scratched.

We are attaching photographs of the damaged items as evidence for our complaint.
As you can see from the photos, the damages were obviously caused by faulty packing and insufficient labelling. The parcels did neither carry a label nor a handling sign indicating "fragile". Moreover, the padding in the particular parcels was almost completely missing.

As bottling of the perfume is scheduled for next week, please arrange the immediate shipment of the replacement at your expense.

Regarding the faulty articles, we are keeping them in our warehouse awaiting your instructions.

We look forward to your soon reply.

Yours sincerely
Bruce Haven
Purchasing Manager

FragranceMakers
102-104 Barlow Road * Cheshire, CW7 2RB
Phone: 0044(0)1606-874589 * Fax: 0044(0)1606-874590

WORD BANK

apology	Entschuldigung
breakage	Bruch
complaint	Beschwerde
evidence	Beweis
faulty	fehlerhaft
insufficient	unzureichend
imprint	Eindruck
jar	Glas(gefäß)
padding	Auspolsterung, Füllmaterial
replacement	Ersatz
scratched	verkratzt

5.7.3. LISTENING FOR GIST

Listen to the telephone conversation and make notes.

What is Mr Brandt's problem?	What does Ms Wise find out?	How does Ms Wise solve the problem?

5.7.4. LISTENING FOR DETAIL

Listen to the conversation again and complete the sentences with the expressions from the box.

my records | place of destination | regret | at the latest | highly important | accept our apologies | rely on | delivery note | before | DE-76934 | express delivery | see to it | misaddressed | key it in

1. Could you please give me the number of the (1) ______________ .
2. Just a moment, I have to check (2) ______________ . Okay, here we are, the delivery note number is (3) ______________ .
3. I have to (4) ______________ to get the details of the delivery.
4. The first consignment went to the correct address while the second one was (5) ______________ .
5. Actually, we need them immediately, Ms Wise, by Friday (6) ______________ as I have promised them to one of our (7) ______________ customers.
6. Okay, I'll (8) ______________ that another consignment will be sent to your correct address by (9) ______________ . Usually, it takes 1 to 2 days to arrive at the (10) ______________ .
7. I think you should receive the goods (11) ______________ Friday.
8. I (12) ______________ having caused you such trouble.
9. I'll (13) ______________ you and expect the delivery before Friday then.
10. Certainly Mr Brandt, and once again, please (14) ______________ for this mistake.

5.7.5. WRITING

You work for *Canny Ltd.*, a producer of canned food, located in 127 Highhill Road, Glasgow G2 7 DL. Your boss has asked you to write a reply to a complaint to Mr Gordon Splash of *Golden Knife*, a catering company. The address of *Golden Knife* is 87 Victoria Road, Dundee DD1 4DU.

Use these notes and the following sample of a reply to a complaint to compose your letter:

- refer to order No. GS-459
- thank for the message of 18 October and the information that the canned tomatoes have not been delivered yet
- you found out that the delay is due to a defect of the can closing machine
- you have arranged for immediate delivery
- to make up for the inconvenience you include a sample of the premium class tomato soup
- apologize for the inconvenience caused
- close the letter

Example of a reply to a complaint

The Textile Company

308 Morgan Street, London WIA 3B2
Phone 071 288 5689 Fax 071 288 5680

www.textile.company.co.uk

4 September 20__

Ms Judith Sorento
Belevue Hotel
144 Seaside Road
Brighton
BN 1 1NS

Dear Mr Stone

Order No St-9015

Thank you for your message of 3 September 20__ in which you informed us about the wrong content of parcel No. 9 of the consignment we sent to you last week.

We have checked the matter and found out that in fact this parcel was originally intended to go to a different customer and therefore contained cutlery instead of sun shades.

I have already arranged for express delivery of the correct articles which should reach you tomorrow. As a small compensation for the mistake, we have included 3 table-cloths which go very well with the ordered sun shades.

Would you please be so kind and return the cutlery to our warehouse carriage forward.

Please accept our apology for the inconvenience you had due to the wrong consignment.

We look forward to doing further business with you.

Yours sincerely

Nigel Fox
Sales Department

5.7.6. CROSSWORD

Complete the crossword.

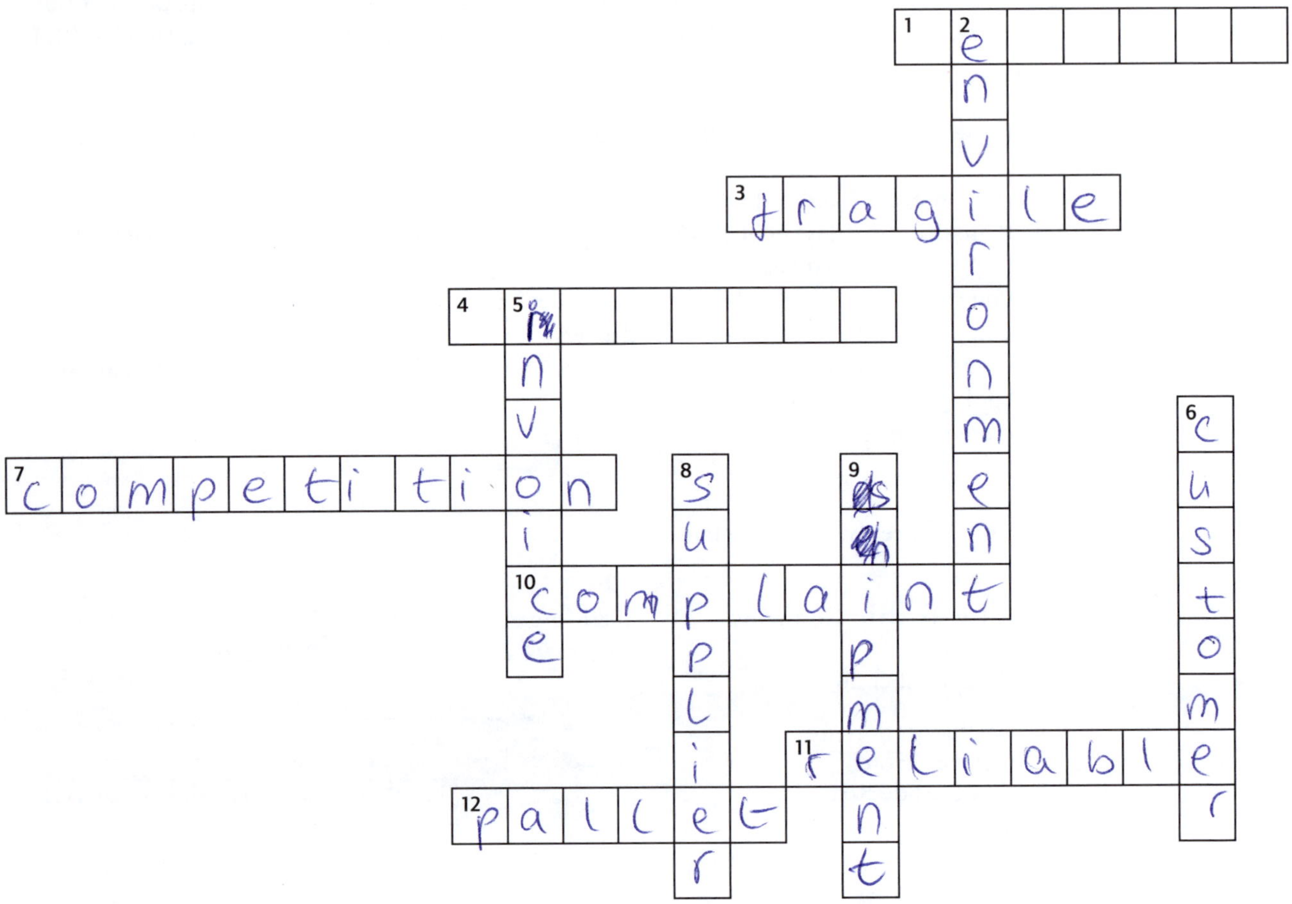

ACROSS

1. Umsatz
3. zerbrechlich
4. verschicken
7. Wettbewerb
10. Beschwerde
11. zuverlässig
12. Palette

DOWN

2. Umwelt
5. Rechnung
6. Kunde
8. Zulieferer
9. Lieferung

Für die englische Lautschrift wurden die phonetischen Zeichen des IPA (International Phonetic Alphabet) verwendet.

Vokale und Diphthonge		Konsonanten	
ɪ	sit	p	pen
e	best	b	bus
æ	cat	t	time
ɒBE	pot	d	do
ʌ	much	k	cat
ʊ	book	g	girl
ə	about	f	fall
i	happy	v	very
u	annual	θ	think
iː	see	ð	this
ɑː	card	s	soft
ɔː	saw	z	zoo
uː	too	ʃ	show
ɜː	bird	ʒ	vision
eɪ	date	h	hot
aɪ	my	tʃ	chip
ɔɪ	boy	dʒ	juice
əʊBE	go	m	man
aʊ	house	n	not
ʊəBE	sure	ŋ	ring
eəBE	hair	l	let
ɪəBE	real	w	why
		r	right
		j	yes

Die dargestellte Lautschrift gibt grundsätzlich die britische Aussprache wieder. Die in Klammern stehenden Lautsymbole (ə) und (r) werden, abhängig vom englischen Sprachraum, ausgesprochen oder nicht. Im amerikanischen Englisch wird (r) üblicherweise mit ausgesprochen.

In der Lautschrift werden zwei Betonungszeichen benutzt, die kennzeichnen, welche Silbe bzw. welcher Wortteil betont werden muss. ˈ bestimmt den Hauptton, ˌ den schwächeren Ton.

UNIT 1

WORD BANK 1

apprenticeship	[ə'prentɪʃɪp]	Ausbildungsplatz
employee	[ˌemplɔɪ'i]	Mitarbeiter
goods issue	[gʊdz 'ɪʃju:]	Warenausgang
goods receipt	[gʊdz rɪ'si:t]	Wareneingang
location	[ləʊ'keɪʃn]	Standort
stock	[stɒk]	Lager
warehouse administration	['weəhaʊz ədˌmɪnɪ'streɪʃn]	Lagerverwaltung
warehouse operator	['weəhaʊz 'ɒpəreɪtə]	Fachlagerist
warehouse supervisor	['weəhaʊz 'su:pəvaɪzə]	Lagerleiter
workplace	['wɜ:k'pleɪs]	Arbeitsplatz

WORD BANK 2

customised	['kʌstømaɪzd]	kundenspezifisch
dedicated	['dedɪkeɪtɪd]	engagiert
groceries	['grəʊsərɪz]	Lebensmittel
organic food	[ɔ:'gænɪk fu:d]	Biolebensmittel
to provide with	[prə'vaɪd wɪð]	versorgen mit
to purchase	[pɜ:tʃəs]	(ein)kaufen
resource	[rɪ'sɔ:s]	Mittel
retail	[ri:'teɪl]	Einzelhandel
staff	[sta:f]	Belegschaft, Mitarbeiter
success	[sək'ses]	Erfolg
support	[sə'pɔ:t]	Unterstützung
wholesaler	['həʊlˌseɪlə]	Großhändler

WORD BANK 3

to arrange	[ə'reɪndʒ]	ausmachen, arrangieren
to be tied up	[bi: taɪd ʌp]	beschäftigt sein
briefing	[bri:fɪŋ]	Einsatzbesprechung
demanding	[dɪ'ma:ndɪŋ]	fordernd
engineer	[ˌendʒɪ'bɪə]	Techniker
to look forward to doing sth.	[lʊk 'fɔ:wəd tu:]	sich darauf freuen, etwas zu tun
to manage sth.	['mænɪdʒ]	es schaffen, etwas zu tun
schedule	['skedju:l]	Zeitplan
smoothly	[smu:ðlɪ]	glatt, ohne Probleme
to suggest	[sə'dʒest]	vorschlagen
vacancy	['veɪkənsɪ]	offene Arbeitsstelle

UNIT 2

WORD BANK 1

ankle	['æŋkl]	Fußgelenk, Fußknöchel
to become familiar with sth.	[bɪ'kʌm fə'ŋɪljə wɪð]	mit etwas vertraut werden
bruise	[brɔu:z]	Prellung, Bluterguss
compensation	[ˌkɑmpen'seɪʃn]	Schmerzensgeld, Schadensersatz
concrete floor	[[kən'kri:t flɔ:]	Betonboden
to crush	[krʌʃ]	quetschen, zerdrücken
fatality	[fə'tælətɪ]	Unglück, Todesfall
fireproof	['faɪəpru:f]	feuerfest, feuerbeständig
hazard	['hæzəd]	Gefahr, Risiko
injury	['ɪndʒərɪ]	Verwundung, Verletzung
to kneel down	[ni:l daʊn]	sich hinknien

measure	[ˌmeʒə]	Maßnahme
to occur	[ə'kɜ:]	auftreten
precautions	[prɪ'kɔ:ʃnz]	Vorsichtsmaßnahmen
to prohibit	[prə'hɪbɪt]	verbieten
severe	[sɪ'vɪə]	ernst, schlimm, schwer
slips and trips	[slɪps ænd trɪps]	Ausrutschen und Stolpern
theft	[θeft]	Diebstahl
threat	[θret]	Drohung, Gefährdung

WORD BANK 2

ample	['æmpl]	geräumig, ausgiebig
to avoid	[ə'vɔɪd]	verhindern
to bump into sth./so.	[bʌmp 'ɪntʊ]	mit etwas/jemandem zusammenstoßen
common	['kɒmən]	alltäglich, häufig, bekannt
entire	[ɪn'taɪə]	ganz, komplett
to exceed	[ɪk'si:d]	übertreffen
inspection	[ɪn´spekʃən]	Prüfung, Kontrolle
manual handling	['mænjʊəl 'hændlɪŋ]	manuelle Handhabung
novice	['nɒvɪs]	Anfänger, Neuling
odd	[ɒd]	seltsam
to pinpoint	['pɪnpɔɪnt]	genau bestimmen, festlegen
posture	['pɒstʃə]	Haltung, Körperhaltung

WORD BANK 3

delivery date	[dɪ'lɪvərɪ deɪt]	Liefertermin
discount	['dɪskaʊnt]	Rabatt, Ermäßigung
to grant	[grɑ:nt]	gewähren, einräumen
grateful	['greɪtfʊl]	dankbar
range of	[reɪndʒ əv]	Auswahl/Angebot an
to rephrase	[rɪ'freɪz]	umformulieren
requirement	[rɪ'kwaɪəmənt]	Anforderung
substantial	[səb'stænʃl]	umfangreich, beträchtlich
terms of delivery	[tɜ:mz əv dɪ'lɪvərɪ]	Lieferbedingungen
terms of payment	[tɜ:mz əv 'peɪmənt]	Zahlungsbedingungen

UNIT 3

WORD BANK 1

apparently	[ə'pærəntlɪ]	anscheinend, augenscheinlich
to check	[tʃæk]	prüfen
condition	[kən'dɪʃn]	Zustand
delivery note	[dɪ'lɪvərɪ nəʊt]	Lieferschein
to document	['dɒkjʊmənt]	beurkunden, dokumentieren
to exchange sth.	[ɪks'tʃeɪndʒ]	etwas austauschen
offer	['ɒfə]	Angebot
order	['ɔ:də]	Auftrag
purchasing department	['pɜ:tʃəsɪŋ dɪ'pɑ:tmənt]	Einkaufsabteilung
reusable	[ˌri:'ju:səbl]	wieder verwendbar, Mehrweg-
to sign a receipt	[saɪn ə rɪ'si:t]	eine Quittung unterschreiben
stock list	['stɒk lɪst]	Lagerliste
to unload sth.	[ˌʌn'ləʊd]	etwas abladen

WORD BANK 2

accounting	[ə'kaʊntɪŋ]	Buchhaltung
air waybill	['eə weɪbɪl]	Luftfrachtbrief
carrier	['kærɪə]	Frachtführer
to complain about	[kəm'pleɪn ə'baʊt]	reklamieren, sich über etwas beschweren
consignment/delivery/ shipment	[kən'saɪnmənt/dɪ'lɪvərɪ/ 'ʃɪpmənt]	Lieferung
to correspond to	[ˌkɒrɪ'spɒnd' tu:]	etwas entsprechen
forwarding documents	['fɔ:wədɪŋ 'dɒkjʊmənts]	Warenbegleitpapiere
goods receipt slip	[gʊdz rɪ'si:t slɪp]	Wareneingangsschein
invoice	['ɪnvɔɪs]	Rechnung
interface	[ˌɪntə'feɪs]	Schnittstelle
in stock	[ɪn stɒk]	auf Lager, vorrätig
packing list	['pækɪŋ lɪst]	Packliste
quality control	['kwɒlətɪ kən'trəʊl]	Qualitätskontrolle

WORD BANK 3

appropriate	[ə'prəʊprɪeɪt]	angemessen
by heart	[baɪ hɑ:t]	auswendig
to consider	[kən'sɪdə]	in Erwägung ziehen, betrachten
favourable	['feɪvərəbl]	günstig
to gain	[geɪn]	erlangen, aneignen
to follow rules/instructions	['fɒləʊ ru:lz/ɪn'strʌkʃənz]	Regeln/Anweisungen befolgen
to omit	[ə'mɪt]	weglassen
to protect from	[prə'tekt frɒm]	schützen vor
vermin	['vɜ:mɪn]	Schädlinge

WORD BANK 4

as a result	[əz ə rɪ'zʌlt]	schlussfolgernd
first of all	[fɜ:st əv ɔ:l]	zuerst, zuallererst
furthermore	[ˌfɜ:ðə'mɔ:]	außerdem, darüber hinaus
in addition	[ɪn ə'dɪʃn]	ergänzend, hinzu kommt
in my opinion	[ɪn maɪ ə'pɪnjən]	meiner Meinung nach
last but not least	[lɑ:st bʌt nɑt li:st]	nicht zuletzt
on the one hand, on the other hand	[ɒn ðə wʌn hænd, ɒn ði: 'ʌðə hænd]	auf der einen Seite, auf der anderen Seite
therefore	['ðeəfɔ:]	somit, deshalb
to sum it up	[tu: sʌm ɪt ʌp]	um es zusammenzufassen
whereas	[weər'æz]	wobei, wohingegen
while	[waɪl]	während

WORD BANK 5

advice	[əd'vaɪs]	Rat, Empfehlung
competitive	[kəm'petətɪv]	wettbewerbsfähig
delivery time	[dɪ'lɪvərɪ 'taɪm]	Lieferzeitpunkt, Lieferfrist
enquiry	[ɪn'kwaɪərɪ]	Anfrage
filing cabinet	['faɪlɪŋ 'kæbɪnɪt]	Aktenschrank
located	[ləʊ'keɪtɪd]	ansässig
luggage	['lʌgɪdʒ]	Gepäck
medium-sized	['mi:djəm saɪzd]	mittelständisch
pallet	['pælɪt]	Palette
to redecorate	[ri:'dekəreɪt]	renovieren

UNIT 4

WORD BANK 1

to become redundant	[bɪ'kʌm rɪ'dʌndənt]	seinen Arbeitsplatz verlieren
to decrease	['di:kri:s]	fallen
(electronic) order picking	[ˌɪlek'trɒnɪk 'ɔ:də 'pɪkɪŋ]	(beleglose) Kommissionierung
to facilitate	[fə'sɪlɪteɪt]	erleichtern
to increase	[ɪn'kri:s]	steigen
logistics	[lə'dʒɪstɪks]	Versorgung, Logistik
low level order picking	[ləʊ ˌlevl' ɔ:də' pɪkɪŋ]	maschinengestützte Kommissionierung
pick-by-barcode	[pɪk baɪ bɑ:kəʊd]	Kommissionieren per Strichcode
pick-by-light	[pɪk baɪ laɪt]	Kommissionieren per LED-Anzeigen
pick-by-vision	[pɪk baɪ 'vɪʒn]	Kommissionieren per Datenbrille
pick-by-voice	[pɪk baɪ vɔɪs]	Kommissionieren per Sprachbefehl
order picking by pick list	['ɔ:də 'pɪkɪŋ baɪ pɪk lɪst]	beleghafte Kommissionierung
time consuming	[taɪm kən'sju:mɪŋ]	zeitaufwändig

WORD BANK 2

aisle	[aɪl]	Gang, Mittelgang
articulated forklift truck	[ɑ:'tɪkjʊleɪt fɔ:klɪft trʌk]	Gelenk-Hubwagen
bay	[beɪ]	Bucht, Laderaum
brand	[brænd]	Markenzeichen
to dispatch	[dɪ'spætʃ]	verschicken
narrow	['nærəʊ]	eng, schmal
peak period	[pi:k pɪərɪəd]	Spitzenzeit
stocktaking	['stɒkˌteɪkɪŋ]	Inventur
storage area	['stɔ:rɪdʒ 'eərɪə]	Lagerfläche
trailer	[treɪlə]	Container, Anhänger
to undertake	[ˌʌndə'teɪk]	abwickeln, ausführen

WORD BANK 3

convenience	[kən'vi:njəns]	Bequemlichkeit, Verbraucherfreundlichkeit
to dispense	[dɪ'spens]	entnehmen
distribution	['dɪstrɪbju:ʃn]	Versand
to encourage	[ɪn'kʌrɪdʒ]	ermuntern
label	['leɪbl]	Etikett, Aufkleber
marketer	['mɑ:kɪtə]	Vermarkter
point of sale	[pɔɪnt əv seɪl]	Kasse, Verkaufsplatz
to preserve sth.	[prɪ'zɜ:v]	etwas aufbewahren
to reuse	[ˌri'ju:s]	wiederverwenden
to sell	[sel]	verkaufen
to stack	[stæk]	aufschichten, stapeln
stress	[stres]	Belastung, Druck
storage	['stɔ:rɪdʒ]	Einlagerung

WORD BANK 4

can	[kæn]	Dose
to confront sth.	[kən'frʌnt]	etwas gegenüberstehen
consumption	[kən'sʌmpʃn]	Verbrauch
to contribute	[kən'trɪbju:t]	beisteuern, einen Beitrag leisten
to dispose	[dɪ'spəʊz]	entsorgen
essential	[ɪ'senʃl]	notwendig, grundlegend

iron ore	['aɪən ɔ:]	Eisenerz
life cycle	['laɪf 'sʌɪkl]	Lebensdauer
to maintain sth.	[meɪn'teɪn]	etwas aufrecht erhalten
processing	['prəʊsesɪŋ]	Bearbeitung, Verarbeitung
shelf life	[ʃelf laɪf]	Haltbarkeit
social benefit	['səʊʃl 'benɪfɪt]	gesellschaftlicher Nutzen
sustainability	[sə'steɪnə'bɪlətɪ]	Nachhaltigkeit

WORD BANK 5

to be affected	[bi: ə'fektɪd]	beeinflusst werden
confirmation	[ˌkɑnfə'meɪʃn]	Bestätigung
free domicile	[fri: 'dɑmɪsaɪl]	frei Haus
quotation	[kwəʊ'teɪʃn]	Preisangebot
recipient	[rɪ'sɪpɪənt]	Abnehmer, Empfänger
storage capacity	['stɔ:rɪdʒ kə'pæsətɪ]	Lagerkapazität

UNIT 5

WORD BANK 1

abroad	[ə'brɔ:d]	Ausland, ins Ausland
to depend on	[dɪ'pend ɒn]	abhängig sein von
exploitation	[ˌeksplɒɪ'teɪʃn]	Ausbeutung, Ausnutzung
extent	[ɪk'stent]	Ausmaß, Umfang
feature	['fi:tʃə]	Merkmal
Gross Domestic Product (GPD)	[grəʊs dəʊ'mestɪk 'prɒdʌkt]	Bruttoinlandsprodukt
interdependence	[ˌɪntədɪ'pendəns]	Abhängigkeit, Wechselbeziehung
literally	['lɪtərəlɪ]	wortwörtlich
origin	['ɒrɪdʒɪn]	Ursprung
to outsource	['aʊtsɔ:s]	ausgliedern
questionnaire	[ˌkwestʃə'neə]	Fragebogen
to set up	[set ʌp]	arrangieren
to shift	[ʃɪft]	verlagern
shortage	['ʃɔ:tɪdʒ]	Mangel
to span	[spæn]	umfassen, umspannen

WORD BANK 2

containerisation	[kən'teɪnəri:seɪʃn]	Container-Transport
corporate image	['kɔ:pərət 'ɪmɪdʒ]	Firmenbild
decade	['dekeɪd]	Jahrzehnt
to perform	[pə'fɔ:m]	auftreten, durchführen
revenue	['revənju:]	Umsatz
to take advantage of	[teɪk əd'vɑ:ntɪdʒ əv]	einen Vorteil aus etwas ziehen
trade barrier	[treɪd 'bærɪə]	Handelsschranke
transport operator	['trænsɔ:t 'ɒpəreɪtə]	Transportunternehmer
ultimate goal	['ʌltɪmət gəʊl]	Endziel

WORD BANK 3

to accompany	[ə'kʌmpənɪ]	begleiten, beifügen
bill of lading	[bɪl əv 'leɪdɪŋ]	Frachtbrief
commercial invoice	[kə'mɜ:ʃl 'ɪnvɔɪs]	Warenrechnung
freight forwarder	[freɪt 'fɔ:wədə]	Spediteur
grade	[greɪd]	Grad, Anspruchsklasse
parcel label	['pɑ:sl leɪbl]	Paketaufkleber
proof	[pru:f]	Beweis, Abzug

to reject	['ri:dʒekt]	abweisen, ablehnen
seagoing vessel	['si:ˌgəʊɪŋ 'vesl]	Seeschiff
to serve	[sɜ:v]	dienen, nützen

WORD BANK 4

apology	[ə'pɒlədʒɪ]	Entschuldigung
breakage	['breɪkɪdʒ]	Bruch
complaint	[kəm'pleɪnt]	Beschwerde
evidence	['evɪdəns]	Beweis
faulty	['fɔ:ltɪ]	fehlerhaft
imprint	[ɪm'prɪnt]	Eindruck, Abdruck
insufficient	[ˌɪnsə'fɪʃnt]	unzureichend
jar	[dʒɑ:]	Glas(gefäß)
padding	['pædɪŋ]	Auspolsterung, Füllmaterial
replacement	[rɪ'pleɪsmənt]	Ersatz
scratched	[skrætʃt]	verkratzt

Alphabetical Wordlist: English-German

A

abroad [ə'brɔ:d] 4	Ausland, ins Ausland
to accompany [ə'kʌmpənɪ] 5	begleiten, beifügen
accounting department [ə'kaʊntɪŋ dɪ'pɑ:tmənt] 3	Buchhaltung
adjustment [ə'dʒʌstmənt] 5	Anpassung, Schadensregelung
advice [əd'vaɪs] 3	Rat, Empfehlung
air waybill ['eə weɪbɪl] 3	Luftfrachtbrief
aisle [aɪl] 4	Gang, Mittelgang
ample ['æmpl] 2	geräumig, ausgiebig
ankle ['æŋkl] 2	Fußgelenk, Fußknöchel
apology [ə'pɒlədʒɪ] 5	Entschuldigung
apparently [ə'pærəntlɪ] 3	anscheinend, augenscheinlich
to appreciate [ə'pri:ʃɪeɪt] 4	zu schätzen wissen, begrüßen
apprentice [ə'prentɪs] 1	Auszubildende(r), Lehrling
apprenticeship [ə'prentɪʃɪp] 1	Ausbildungsplatz
appropriate [ə'prəʊprɪeɪt] 3	angemessen
to arrange [ə'reɪndʒ] 1	ausmachen, arrangieren
articulated forklift truck [ɑ:'tɪkjʊleɪt fɔ:klɪft trʌk] 4	Gelenk-Hubwagen
as a result [əz ə rɪ'zʌlt] 3	schlussfolgernd
to avoid [ə'vɔɪd] 2	verhindern

B

bay [beɪ] 4	Bucht, Laderaum
to be affected [bi: ə'fektɪd] 4	beeinflusst werden
to be tied up [bi: taɪd ʌp] 1	beschäftigt sein
to become familiar with [bɪ'kʌm fə'ŋɪljə wɪð] 2	mit etwas vertraut werden
to become redundant [bɪ'kʌm rɪ'dʌndənt] 4	seinen Arbeitsplatz verlieren
bill of lading [bɪl əv 'leɪdɪŋ] 5	Frachtbrief
brand [brænd] 4	Markenzeichen
breakage ['breɪkɪdʒ] 5	Bruch
briefing [bri:fɪŋ] 1	Einsatzbesprechung
bruise [brəu:z] 2	Prellung, Bluterguss

to bump into sth./so. [bʌmp 'ɪntʊ] 2	mit etwas/jemandem zusammenstoßen
by heart [baɪ hɑ:t] 3	auswendig

C

can [kæn] 4	Dose
carrier ['kærɪə] 3	Frachtführer
to check [tʃæk] 3	prüfen
commercial invoice [kə'mɜ:ʃl 'ɪnvɔɪs] 5	Warenrechnung
common ['kɒmən] 2	alltäglich, häufig, bekannt
compensation [ˌkɑmpen'seɪʃn] 2	Schmerzensgeld, Schadensersatz
competition [ˌkɒmpɪ'tɪʃn] 5	Wettbewerb
competitive [kəm'petətɪv] 3	wettbewerbsfähig
to complain [kəm'pleɪn] 3	reklamieren, sich beschweren
complaint [kəm'pleɪnt] 5	Beschwerde
concrete floor [kən'kri:t flɔ:] 2	Betonboden
condition [kən'dɪʃn] 3	Zustand
confirmation [ˌkɑnfə'meɪʃn] 4	Bestätigung
to confront sth. [kən'frʌntɪd] 4	etwas gegenüberstehen
to consider [kən'sɪdə] 3	in Erwägung ziehen, betrachten
consignment/delivery/shipment [kən'saɪnmənt/dɪ'lɪvərɪ/'ʃɪpmənt] 3	Lieferung
consumption [kən'sʌmpʃn] 4	Verbrauch
containerisation [kən'teɪnəri:seɪʃn] 5	Container-Transport
to contribute [kən'trɪbju:t] 4	beisteuern, einen Beitrag leisten
convenience [kən'vi:njəns] 4	Bequemlichkeit, Verbraucherfreundlichkeit
corporate image ['kɔ:pərət 'ɪmɪdʒ] 5	Firmenbild
to correspond [ˌkɒrɪ'spɒnd' tu:] 3	etwas entsprechen
to crush [krʌʃ] 2	quetschen, zerdrücken
customised ['kʌstømaɪzd] 1	kundenspezifisch
cutlery ['kʌtlərɪ] 5	Besteck

D

decade ['dekeɪd] 5	Jahrzehnt
to decrease ['di:kri:s] 4	fallen
dedicated ['dedɪkeɪtɪd] 1	engagiert
delicate ['delɪkət] 5	heikel
delivery date [dɪ'lɪvərɪ deɪt] 2	Liefertermin
delivery note [dɪ'lɪvərɪ nəʊt] 3	Lieferschein
delivery time [dɪ'lɪvərɪ'taɪm] 3	Lieferzeitpunkt, Lieferfrist
demanding [dɪ'mɑ:ndɪŋ] 1	fordernd
to depend on [dɪ'pend ɒn] 5	abhängig sein von
discount ['dɪskaʊnt] 2	Rabatt, Ermäßigung
to dispatch [dɪ'spætʃ] 4	verschicken
to dispense [dɪ'spens] 4	entnehmen
to dispose [dɪ'spəʊz] 4	entsorgen
distribution ['dɪstrɪbju:tɪŋ] 4	Versand
to document ['dɒkjʊmənt] 3	beurkunden, dokumentieren

E

to effect [ɪ'fekt] 4	ausführen, durchführen
(electronic) order picking [ˌɪlek'trɒnɪk 'ɔ:də 'pɪkɪŋ] 4	(beleglose) Kommisionierung
employee [ˌemplɔɪ'i] 1	Mitarbeiter
employer [ɪm'plɔɪə] 1	Arbeitgeber
to encourage [ɪn'kʌrɪdʒ] 4	ermuntern
engineer [ˌendʒɪ'bɪə] 1	Techniker

enquiry [ɪn'kwaɪərɪ] 3	Anfrage
entire [ɪn'taɪəstɑ:f] 2	ganz, komplett
essential [ɪ'senʃl] 4	notwendig, grundlegend
evidence ['evɪdəns] 5	Beweis
to exceed [ɪk'si:d] 2	übertreffen
to exchange sth. [ɪks'tʃeɪndʒ] 3	etwas austauschen
expectation [ˌekspek'teɪzn] 5	Erwartung
exploitation [ˌeksplɒɪ'teɪʃn] 5	Ausbeutung, Ausnutzung
extent [ɪk'stent] 5	Ausmaß, Umfang

F

to facilitate [fə'sɪlɪteɪt] 4	erleichtern
fatality [fə'tælətɪ] 2	Unglück, Todesfall
faulty ['fɔ:ltɪ] 5	fehlerhaft
favourable ['feɪvərəbl] 3	günstig
feature ['fi:tʃə] 5	Merkmal
filing cabinet ['faɪlɪŋ 'kæbɪnɪt] 3	Aktenschrank
fireproof ['faɪəpru:f] 2	feuerfest, feuerbeständig
first of all [fɜ:st əv ɔ:l] 3	zuerst, zuallererst
forwarding documents ['fɔ:wədɪŋ 'dɒkjʊmənts] 3	Warenbegleitpapiere
free domicile [fri: 'dɑmɪsaɪl] 4	frei Haus
freight forwarder [freɪt 'fɔ:wədə] 5	Spediteur
furthermore [ˌfɜ:ðə'mɔ:] 3	außerdem, darüber hinaus

G/H

to gain [geɪn] 3	erlangen, aneignen
goods issue [gʊdz 'ɪʃju:] 1	Warenausgang
goods receipt [gʊdz rɪ'si:t] 1	Wareneingang
goods receipt slip [gʊdz rɪ'si:t slɪp] 3	Wareneingangsschein
grade [greɪd] 5	Grad, Anspruchsklasse
to grant [grɑ:nt] 2	gewähren, einräumen
grateful ['greɪtfʊl] 2	dankbar
groceries ['grəʊsərɪz] 1	Lebensmittel
Gross Domestic Product (GPD) [grəʊs dəʊ'mestɪk 'prɒdʌkt] 5	Bruttoinlandsprodukt
hazard ['hæzəd] 2	Gefahr, Risiko

I/J/K

impact ['ɪmpækt] 5	Einfluss, Auswirkung
imprint [ɪm'prɪnt] 5	Eindruck, Abdruck
in addition [ɪn ə'dɪʃn] 3	ergänzend, hinzu kommt
in my opinion [ɪn maɪ ə'pɪnjən] 3	meiner Meinung nach
inconvenience [ˌɪnkən'vi:njəns] 5	Unannehmlichkeit
to increase [ɪn'kri:s] 4	steigen
injury ['ɪndʒərɪ] 2	Verwundung, Verletzung
inspection [ɪn´spekʃən] 2	Prüfung, Kontrolle
in stock [ɪn stɒk] 3	auf Lager, vorrätig
insufficient [ˌɪnsə'fɪʃnt] 5	unzureichend
interdependence [ˌɪntədɪ'pendəns] 5	Abhängigkeit, Wechselbeziehung
interface [ˌɪntə'feɪs] 3	Schnittstelle
invoice ['ɪnvɔɪs] 3	Rechnung
iron ore ['aɪən ɔ:] 4	Eisenerz
issue ['ɪʃu:] 5	Angelegenheit
jar [dʒɑ:] 5	Glas(gefäß)
to kneel down [ni:l daʊn] 2	sich hinknien

L

label ['leɪbl] 4	Etikett, Aufkleber
last but not least [lɑ:st bʌt nɑt li:st] 3	nicht zuletzt
life cycle ['laɪf 'sʌɪkl] 4	Lebensdauer
literally ['lɪtərəlɪ] 5	wortwörtlich
located [ləʊ'keɪtɪd] 3	ansässig
location [ləʊ'keɪʃn] 1	Standort
logistics [lə'dʒɪstɪks] 4	Versorgung, Logistik
to look forward to doing sth. [lʊk 'fɔ:wəd tu:] 1	sich darauf freuen, etwas zu tun
low level order picking [ləʊ ˌlevl' ɔ:də' pɪkɪŋ] 4	maschinengestützte Kommissionierung
luggage ['lʌgɪdʒ] 3	Gepäck

M/N

to maintain sth. [meɪn'teɪn] 4	etwas aufrecht erhalten
to manage sth. ['mænɪdʒ] 1	es schaffen, etwas zu tun
mandatory ['mændətərɪ] 2	verpflichtend
manual handling ['mænjʊəl 'hændlɪŋ] 2	manuelle Handhabung
marketer ['mɑ:kɪtə] 4	Vermarkter
measure [ˌmeʒə] 2	Maßnahme
medium-sized ['mi:djəm saɪzd] 3	mittelständisch
narrow ['nærəʊ] 4	eng, schmal
novice ['nɒvɪs] 2	Anfänger, Neuling

O

to obey [ə'beɪ] 3	befolgen, gehorchen
to occur [ə'kɜ:] 2	auftreten
odd [ɒd] 2	seltsam
offer ['ɒfə] 3	Angebot
to omit [ə'mɪt] 3	weglassen
on the one hand, on the other hand [ɒn ðə wʌn hænd, ɒn ði: 'ʌðə hænd] 3	auf der einen Seite, auf der anderen Seite
order ['ɔ:də] 3	Auftrag
order picking by pick list ['ɔ:də 'pɪkɪŋ baɪ pɪk lɪst] 4	beleghafte Kommissionierung
organic food [ɔ:'gænɪk fu:d] 1	Biolebensmittel
origin ['ɒrɪdʒɪn] 5	Ursprung
to outsource ['aʊtsɔ:s] 5	ausgliedern

P/Q

packing list ['pækɪŋ lɪst] 3	Packliste
padding ['pædɪŋ] 5	Auspolsterung, Füllmaterial
pallet ['pælɪt] 3	Palette
parcel label ['pɑ:sl leɪbl] 5	Paketaufkleber
peak period [pi:k pɪərɪəd] 4	Spitzenzeit
to perform [pə'fɔ:m] 5	auftreten, durchführen
pick-by-barcode [pɪk baɪ bɑ:kəʊd] 4	Kommissionieren per Strichcode
pick-by-light [pɪk baɪ laɪt] 4	Kommissionieren per LED-Anzeige
pick-by-vision [pɪkbaɪ'vɪʒn] 4	Kommissionieren per Datenbrille
pick-by-voice [pɪk baɪ vɔɪs] 4	Kommissionieren per Sprachbefehl
to pinpoint ['pɪnpɔɪnt] 2	genau bestimmen, festlegen
point of sale [pɔɪnt əv seɪl] 4	Kasse, Verkaufsplatz
posture ['pɒstʃə] 2	Haltung, Körperhaltung
precautions [prɪ'kɔ:ʃnz] 2	Vorsichtsmaßnahmen
to preserve sth. [prɪ'zɜ:v] 4	etwas aufbewahren
processing ['prəʊsesɪŋ] 4	Bearbeitung, Verarbeitung
to prohibit [prə'hɪbɪt] 2	verbieten

proof [pru:f] 5	Beweis, Abzug
to protect from [prə'tekt frɒm] 3	schützen vor
to provide with [prə'vaɪd wɪð] 1	versorgen mit
to purchase [pɜ:tʃəs] 1	(ein)kaufen
purchasing department ['pɜ:tʃəsɪŋ dɪ'pɑ:tmənt] 3	Einkaufsabteilung
quality control department ['kwɒlətɪ kən'trəʊl dɪ'pɑ:tmənt] 3	Qualitätskontrolle
questionnaire [,kwestʃə'neə] 5	Fragebogen
quotation [kwəʊ'teɪʃn] 4	Preisangebot

R

range of [reɪndʒ əv] 2	Auswahl/Angebot an
reasonable ['ri:znəbl] 1	vernünftig
receipt [rɪ'si:t] 4	Erhalt, Eingang
recipient [rɪ'sɪpɪənt] 4	Abnehmer, Empfänger
to redecorate [ri:'dekəreɪt] 3	renovieren
to reject ['ri:dʒekt] 5	abweisen, ablehnen
to rephrase [rɪ'freɪz] 2	umformulieren
replacement [rɪ'pleɪsmənt] 5	Ersatz
requirement [rɪ'kwaɪəmənt] 2	Anforderung
resource [rɪ'sɔ:s] 1	Mittel
retail [ri:'teɪl] 1	Einzelhandel
reusable [,ri:'ju:səbl] 3	wieder verwendbar, Mehrweg-
to reuse [,ri'ju:s] 4	wiederverwenden
revenue ['revənju:] 5	Umsatz

S

satisfactory [,sætɪs'fæktərɪ] 4	zufriedenstellend
schedule ['skedju:l] 1	Zeitplan
scratched [skrætʃt] 5	verkratzt
seagoing vessel ['si:,gəʊɪŋ 'vesl] 5	Seeschiff
to sell [sel] 4	verkaufen
to serve [sɜ:v] 5	dienen, nützen
to set up [set ʌp] 5	arrangieren
severe [sɪ'vɪə] 2	ernst, schlimm, schwer
shelf life [ʃelf laɪf] 4	Haltbarkeit
to shift [ʃɪft] 5	verlagern
shortage ['ʃɔ:tɪdʒ] 5	Mangel
to sign a receipt [saɪn ə rɪ'si:t] 3	eine Quittung unterschreiben
slips and trips [slɪps ænd trɪps] 2	Ausrutschen und Stolpern
smoothly [smu:ðlɪ] 1	glatt, ohne Probleme
social benefit ['səʊʃl 'benɪfɪt] 4	gesellschaftlicher Nutzen
to span [spæn] 5	umfassen, umspannen
to stack [stæk] 4	aufschichten, stapeln
staff [sta:f] 1	Belegschaft, Mitarbeiter
stock [stɒk] 1	Lager
stock list ['stɒk lɪst] 3	Lagerliste
stocktaking ['stɒk,teɪkɪŋ] 4	Inventur
storage ['stɔ:rɪdʒ] 4	Einlagerung
storage area ['stɔ:rɪdʒ 'eərɪə] 4	Lagerfläche
storage capacity ['stɔ:rɪdʒ kə'pæsətɪ] 4	Lagerkapazität
stress [stres] 4	Belastung, Druck
to submit [səb'mɪt] 4	unterbreiten
subsidiary [səb'sɪdjərɪ] 1	Niederlassung
substantial [səb'stænʃl] 2	umfangreich, beträchtlich
success [sək'ses] 1	Erfolg

to suggest [sə'dʒest] 1	vorschlagen
to sum it up [sʌm ɪt ʌp] 3	um es zusammenzufassen
support [sə'pɔ:t] 1	Unterstützung
sustainability [sə'steɪnə'bɪlətɪ] 4	Nachhaltigkeit

T

to take advantage of [teɪk əd'vɑ:ntɪdʒ əv] 5	einen Vorteil aus etwas ziehen
terms of delivery [tɜ:mz əv dɪ'lɪvərɪ] 2	Lieferbedingungen
terms of payment [tɜ:mz əv 'peɪmənt] 2	Zahlungsbedingungen
theft [θeft] 2	Diebstahl
therefore ['ðeəfɔ:] 3	somit, deshalb
threat [θret] 2	Drohung, Gefährdung
time consuming [taɪm kən'sju:mɪŋ] 4	zeitaufwändig
trade barrier [treɪd 'bærɪə] 5	Handelsschranke
trailer [treɪlə] 4	Container, Anhänger
transport operator ['trænsɔ:t 'ɒpəreɪtə] 5	Transportunternehmer

U/V/W

ultimate goal ['ʌltɪmət gəʊl] 5	Endziel
to undertake [ˌʌndə'teɪk] 4	abwickeln, ausführen
to unload sth. [ˌʌn'ləʊd] 3	etwas abladen
vacancy ['veɪkənsɪ] 1	offene Arbeitsstelle
vermin ['vɜ:mɪn] 3	Schädlinge
walk through [wɔ:k θru:] 2	Rundgang, Ortsbesichtigung
warehouse administration ['weəhaʊz ədˌmɪnɪ'streɪʃn] 1	Lagerverwaltung
warehouse operator ['weəhaʊz 'ɒpəreɪtə] 1	Fachlagerist
warehouse supervisor ['weəhaʊz 'su:pəvaɪzə] 1	Lagerleiter
whereas [weər'æz] 3	wobei, wohingegen
while [waɪl] 3	während
wholesaler ['həʊlˌseɪlə] 1	Großhändler
workplace ['wɜ:k'pleɪs] 1	Arbeitsplatz

Alphabetical Wordlist: German-English

A

abhängig sein von	to depend on [dɪ'pend ɒn] 5
Abhängigkeit	interdependence [ˌɪntədɪ'pendəns] 5
abladen: etwas abl.	to unload sth. [ˌʌn'ləʊd] 3
ablehnen	to reject ['ri:dʒekt] 5
Abnehmer	recipient [rɪ'sɪpɪənt] 4
abwickeln	to undertake [ˌʌndə'teɪk] 4
Abzug	proof [pru:f] 5
Aktenschrank	filing cabinet ['faɪlɪŋ 'kæbɪnɪt] 3
alltäglich	common ['kɒmən] 2
Anfänger	novice ['nɒvɪs] 2
Anforderung	requirement [rɪ'kwaɪəmənt] 2
Anfrage	enquiry [ɪn'kwaɪərɪ] 3
Angebot	offer ['ɒfə] 3
Angelegenheit	issue ['ɪʃu:] 5
angemessen	appropriate [ə'prəʊprɪeɪt] 3
Anhänger	trailer [treɪlə] 4
Anpassung	adjustment [ə'dʒʌstmənt] 5

ansässig	located [ləʊ'keɪtɪd] 3
anscheinend	apparently [ə'pærəntlɪ] 3
Arbeitgeber	employer [ɪm'plɔɪə] 1
Arbeitsplatz	workplace ['wɜ:k'pleɪs] 1
arrangieren	to set up [set ʌp] 5, to arrange [ə'reɪndʒ] 1
Aufkleber	label ['leɪbl] 4
auf Lager (vorrätig)	in stock [ɪn stɒk] 3
aufschichten	to stack [stæk] 4
aufrecht erhalten, etwas aufr. erh.	to maintain sth. [meɪn'teɪn] 4
Auftrag	order ['ɔ:də] 3
auftreten	to occur [ə'kɜ:] 2
Ausbeutung	exploitation [ˌeksplɔɪ'teɪʃn] 5
Ausbildungsplatz	apprenticeship [ə'prentɪʃɪp] 1
ausführen	to effect [ɪ'fekt] 4
ausgliedern	to outsource ['aʊtsɔ:s] 5
Ausland, ins Ausland	abroad [ə'brɔ:d] 4
Ausmaß	extent [ɪk'stent] 5
Auspolsterung	padding ['pædɪŋ] 5
Ausrutschen und Stolpern	slips and trips [slɪps ænd trɪps] 2
außerdem	furthermore [ˌfɜ:ðə'mɔ:] 3
Auswahl	range of [reɪndʒ əv] 2
auswendig	by heart [baɪ hɑ:t] 3
Auszubildende(r)	apprentice [ə'prentɪs] 1

B

Bearbeitung	processing ['prəʊsesɪŋ] 4
beeinflusst werden	to be affected [bi: ə'fektɪd] 4
befolgen	to obey [ə'beɪ] 3
begleiten	to accompany [ə'kʌmpənɪ] 5
beisteuern	to contribute [kən'trɪbju:t] 4
Belastung	stress [stres] 4
Belegschaft	staff [stɑ:f] 1
Bequemlichkeit	convenience [kən'vi:njəns] 4
beschäftigt sein	to be tied up [bi: taɪd ʌp] 1
Beschwerde	complaint [kəm'pleɪnt] 5
beschweren: sich beschw.	to complain [kəm'pleɪn] 3
Bestätigung	confirmation [ˌkɑnfə'meɪʃn] 4
Besteck	cutlery ['kʌtlərɪ] 5
Betonboden	concrete floor [kən'kri:t flɔ:] 2
beurkunden	to document ['dɒkjʊmənt] 3
Beweis	evidence ['evɪdəns] 5
Biolebensmittel	organic food [ɔ:'gænɪk fu:d] 1
Bruch	breakage ['breɪkɪdʒ] 5
Bruttoinlandsprodukt	Gross Domestic Product (GPD) [grəʊs dəʊ'mestɪk 'prɒdʌkt] 5
Buchhaltung	accounting department [ə'kaʊntɪŋ dɪ'pɑ:tmənt] 3
Bucht (Laderaum)	bay [beɪ] 4

C/D

Container-Transport	containerisation [kən'teɪnəri:seɪʃn] 5
dankbar	grateful ['greɪtfʊl] 2
Diebstahl	theft [θeft] 2
dienen	to serve [sɜ:v] 5
Dose	can [kæn] 4
Drohung	threat [θret] 2
Druck	stress [stres] 4

E

Eindruck (Abdruck)	imprint [ɪm'prɪnt] 5
Einfluss	impact ['ɪmpækt] 5
Eingang	receipt [rɪ'si:t] 4
Einkaufsabteilung	purchasing department ['pɜ:tʃəsɪŋ dɪ'pɑ:tmənt] 3
Einlagerung	storage ['stɔ:rɪdʒ] 4
Einsatzbesprechung	briefing [bri:fɪŋ] 1
Einzelhandel	retail [ri:'teɪl] 1
Eisenerz	iron ore ['aɪən ɔ:] 4
Empfänger	recipient [rɪ'sɪpɪənt] 4
Endziel	ultimate goal ['ʌltɪmət gəʊl] 5
eng	narrow ['nærəʊ] 4
engagiert	dedicated ['dedɪkeɪtɪd] 1
entnehmen	to dispense [dɪ'spens] 4
Entschuldigung	apology [ə'pɒlədʒɪ] 5
entsorgen	to dispose [dɪ'spəʊz] 4
entsprechen, etwas entspr.	to correspond [ˌkɒrɪ'spɒnd' tu:] 3
Erfolg	success [sək'ses] 1
ergänzend (hinzu kommt)	in addition [ɪn ə'dɪʃn] 3
erlangen	to gain [geɪn] 3
erleichtern	to facilitate [fə'sɪlɪteɪt] 4
ermuntern	to encourage [ɪn'kʌrɪdʒ] 4
ernst	severe [sɪ'vɪə] 2
Ersatz	replacement [rɪ'pleɪsmənt] 5
Erwartung	expectation [ˌekspek'teɪzn] 5
erwägen: in Erwägung ziehen	to consider [kən'sɪdə] 3
Etikett	label ['leɪbl] 4

F

Fachlagerist	warehouse operator ['weəhaʊz 'ɒpəreɪtə] 1
fallen	to decrease ['di:kri:s] 4
fehlerhaft	faulty ['fɔ:ltɪ] 5
festlegen	to pinpoint ['pɪnpɔɪnt] 2
feuerfest, feuerbeständig	fireproof ['faɪəpru:f] 2
Firmenbild	corporate image ['kɔ:pərət 'ɪmɪdʒ] 5
fordernd	demanding [dɪ'mɑ:ndɪŋ] 1
Frachtbrief	bill of lading [bɪl əv 'leɪdɪŋ] 5
Frachtführer	carrier ['kærɪə] 3
Fragebogen	questionnaire [ˌkwestʃə'neə] 5
frei Haus	free domicile [fri: 'dɑmɪsaɪl] 4
Füllmaterial	padding ['pædɪŋ] 5
Fußgelenk, Fußknöchel	ankle ['æŋkl] 2

G

Gang	aisle [aɪl] 4
ganz (komplett)	entire [ɪn'taɪəstɑ:f] 2
Gefahr	hazard ['hæzəd] 2
Gelenk-Hubwagen	articulated forklift [ɑ:'tɪkjʊleɪt fɔ:klɪft trʌk] 4
Gepäck	luggage ['lʌgɪdʒ] 3
geräumig	ample ['æmpl] 2
gewähren	to grant [grɑ:nt] 2
Glas(gefäß)	jar [dʒɑ:] 5
glatt	smoothly [smu:ðlɪ] 1
Grad	grade [greɪd] 5

Großhändler	wholesaler ['həʊl,seɪlə] 1
günstig	favourable ['feɪvərəbl] 3

H

Haltbarkeit	shelf life [ʃelf laɪf] 4
Haltung (Körperhaltung)	posture ['pɒstʃə] 2
Handelsschranke	trade barrier [treɪd 'bærɪə] 5
heikel	delicate ['delɪkət] 5

I/J

Inventur	stocktaking ['stɒk,teɪkɪŋ] 4
Jahrzehnt	decade ['dekeɪd] 5

K

Kasse	point of sale [pɔɪnt əv seɪl] 4
kaufen, einkaufen	to purchase [pɜ:tʃəs] 1
Kommissionieren per Datenbrille	pick-by-vision [pɪkbaɪ'vɪʒn] 4
Kommissionieren per LED-Anzeige	pick-by-light [pɪk baɪ laɪt] 4
Kommissionieren per Sprachbefehl	pick-by-voice [pɪk baɪ vɔɪs] 4
Kommissionieren per Strichcode	pick-by-barcode [pɪk baɪ bɑ:kəʊd] 4
Kommisionierung, beleglose	(electronic) order picking [,ɪlek'trɒnɪk 'ɔ:də 'pɪkɪŋ] 4
kundenspezifisch	customised ['kʌstømaɪzd] 1

L

Lager	stock [stɒk] 1
Lagerfläche	storage area ['stɔ:rɪdʒ 'eərɪə] 4
Lagerkapazität	storage capacity ['stɔ:rɪdʒ kə'pæsətɪ] 4
Lagerleiter	warehouse supervisor ['weəhaʊz 'su:pəvaɪzə] 1
Lagerliste	stock list ['stɒk lɪst] 3
Lagerverwaltung	warehouse administration ['weəhaʊz əd,mɪnɪ'streɪʃn] 1
Lebensdauer	life cycle ['laɪf 'sʌɪkl] 4
Lebensmittel	groceries ['grəʊsərɪz] 1
Lieferbedingungen	terms of delivery [tɜ:mz əv dɪ'lɪvərɪ] 2
Lieferfrist	delivery time [dɪ'lɪvərɪ'taɪm] 3
Lieferschein	delivery note [dɪ'lɪvərɪ nəʊt] 3
Liefertermin	delivery date [dɪ'lɪvərɪ deɪt] 2
Lieferung	consignment/delivery/shipment [kən'saɪnmənt/dɪ'lɪvərɪ/'ʃɪpmənt] 3
Lieferzeitpunkt	delivery time [dɪ'lɪvərɪ'taɪm] 3
Logistik	logistics [lə'dʒɪstɪks] 4
Luftfrachtbrief	air waybill ['eə weɪbɪl] 3

M

Mangel	shortage ['ʃɔ:tɪdʒ] 5
manuelle Handhabung	manual handling ['mænjʊəl 'hændlɪŋ] 2
Markenzeichen	brand [brænd] 4
Maßnahme	measure [,meʒə] 2
Meinung: meiner Meinung nach	in my opinion [ɪn maɪ ə'pɪnjən] 3
Merkmal	feature ['fi:tʃə] 5
Mitarbeiter	employee [,emplɔɪ'i] 1
Mittel	resource [rɪ'sɔ:s] 1
Mittelgang	aisle [aɪl] 4
mittelständisch	medium-sized ['mi:djəm saɪzd] 3

N

Nachhaltigkeit	sustainability [sə'steɪnə'bɪlətɪ] 4
nicht zuletzt	last but not least [lɑ:st bʌt nɑt li:st] 3
Niederlassung	subsidiary [səb'sɪdjərɪ] 1
notwendig (grundlegend)	essential [ɪ'senʃl] 4

O/P

offen: offene Arbeitsstelle	vacancy ['veɪkənsɪ] 1
Packliste	packing list ['pækɪŋ lɪst] 3
Paketaufkleber	parcel label ['pɑ:sl leɪbl] 5
Palette	pallet ['pælɪt] 3
Preisangebot	quotation [kwəʊ'teɪʃn] 4
Prellung	bruise [brɔu:z] 2
prüfen	to check [tʃæk] 3
Prüfung (Kontrolle)	inspection [ɪn´spekʃən] 2

Q/R

Qualitätskontrolle	quality control department ['kwɒlətɪ kən'trəʊl dɪ'pɑ:tmənt] 3
quetschen (zerdrücken)	to crush [krʌʃ] 2
Quittung: eine Qu. unterschreiben	to sign a receipt [saɪn ə rɪ'si:t] 3
Rabatt	discount ['dɪskaʊnt] 2
Rat	advice [əd'vaɪs] 3
Rechnung	invoice ['ɪnvɔɪs] 3
reklamieren	to complain [kəm'pleɪn] 3
renovieren	to redecorate [ri:'dekəreɟt] 3
Rundgang	walk through [wɔ:k θru:] 2

S

Schadensersatz	compensation [ˌkɑmpen'seɪʃn] 2
Schädlinge	vermin ['vɜ:mɪn] 3
schlussfolgernd	as a result [əz ə rɪ'zʌlt] 3
Schnittstelle	interface [ˌɪntə'feɪs] 3
schützen vor	to protect from [prə'tekt frɒm] 3
Seeschiff	seagoing vessel ['si:ˌgəʊɪŋ 'vesl] 5
seltsam	odd [ɒd] 2
sich darauf freuen, etwas zu tun	to look forward to doing sth. [lʊk 'fɔ:wəd tu:] 1
sich hinknien	to kneel down [ni:l daʊn] 2
somit	therefore ['ðeəfɔ:] 3
Spediteur	freight forwarder [freɪt 'fɔ:wədə] 5
Spitzenzeit	peak period [pi:k pɪərɪəd] 4
Standort	location [ləʊ'keɪʃn] 1
stapeln	to stack [stæk] 4
steigen	to increase [ɪn'kri:s] 4

T/U

Techniker	engineer [ˌendʒɪ'bɪə] 1
Transportunternehmer	transport operator ['trænsɔ:t 'ɒpəreɪtə] 5
übertreffen	to exceed [ɪk'si:d] 2
umfangreich (beträchtlich)	substantial [səb'stænʃl] 2
umformulieren	to rephrase [rɪ'freɪz] 2
Umsatz	revenue ['revənju:] 5
umspannen	to span [spæn] 5
Unannehmlichkeit	inconvenience [ˌɪnkən'vi:njəns] 5
Unglück (Todesfall)	fatality [fə'tælətɪ] 2
unterbreiten	to submit [səb'mɪt] 4

Unterstützung	support [sə'pɔ:t] 1
unzureichend	insufficient [ˌɪnsə'fɪʃnt] 5
Ursprung	origin ['ɒrɪdʒɪn] 5

V

verbieten	to prohibit [prə'hɪbɪt] 2
Verbrauch	consumption [kən'sʌmpʃn] 4
Verbraucherfreundlichkeit	convenience [kən'vi:njəns] 4
verhindern	to avoid [ə'vɔɪd] 2
verkaufen	to sell [sel] 4
verkratzt	scratched [skrætʃt] 5
verlagern	to shift [ʃɪft] 5
Vermarkter	marketer ['mɑ:kɪtə] 4
vernünftig	reasonable ['ri:znəbl] 1
verpflichtend	mandatory ['mændətərɪ] 2
Versand	distribution ['dɪstrɪbju:tɪŋ] 4
verschicken	to dispatch [dɪ'spætʃ] 4
versorgen mit	to provide with [prə'vaɪd wɪð] 1
Verwundung (Verletzung)	injury ['ɪndʒərɪ] 2
vorschlagen	to suggest [sə'dʒest] 1
Vorsichtsmaßnahmen	precautions [prɪ'kɔ:ʃnz] 2

W

während	while [waɪl] 3
Warenausgang	goods issue [gʊdz 'ɪʃju:] 1
Warenbegleitpapiere	forwarding documents ['fɔ:wədɪŋ 'dɒkjʊmənts] 3
Wareneingang	goods receipt [gʊdz rɪ'si:t] 1
Wareneingangsschein	goods receipt slip [gʊdz rɪ'si:t slɪp] 3
Warenrechnung	commercial invoice [kə'mɜ:ʃl 'ɪnvɔɪs] 5
weglassen	to omit [ə'mɪt] 3
Wettbewerb	competition [ˌkɒmpɪ'tɪʃn] 5
wettbewerbsfähig	competitive [kəm'petətɪv] 3
wieder verwendbar	reusable [ˌri:'ju:səbl] 3
wiederverwenden	to reuse [ˌri'ju:s] 4
wortwörtlich	literally ['lɪtərəlɪ] 5

Z

Zahlungsbedingungen	terms of payment [tɜ:mz əv 'peɪmənt] 2
zeitaufwändig	time consuming [taɪm kən'sju:mɪŋ] 4
Zeitplan	schedule ['skedju:l] 1
zusammenstoßen: mit etw./jem. z.	to bump into sth./so. [bʌmp 'ɪntʊ] 2
zuerst (zuallererst)	first of all [fɜ:st əv ɔ:l] 3
zufriedenstellend	satisfactory [ˌsætɪs'fæktərɪ] 4
Zustand	condition [kən'dɪʃn] 3

Infinitive	Simple Past	Past Participle	German
arise	arose	arisen	entstehen, sich erheben
be	was/were	been	sein
bear	bore	borne	(er)tragen
beat	beat	beaten, beat	schlagen
become	became	become	werden
begin	began	begun	beginnen
bend	bent	bent	biegen, beugen
bid	bid	bid	bieten, ein Angebot abgeben
bind	bound	bound	binden, verpflichten
break	broke	broken	(zer)brechen
bring	brought	brought	bringen
build	built	built	bauen
burn	burnt, burned	burnt, burned	brennen, verbrennen
burst	burst	burst	platzen
buy	bought	bought	kaufen
catch	caught	caught	fangen
choose	chose	chosen	wählen
come	came	come	kommen
cost	cost	cost	kosten
cut	cut	cut	schneiden
deal	dealt	dealt	handeln, Geschäfte tätigen
do	did	done	tun, machen
draw	drew	drawn	zeichnen
dream	dreamt, dreamed	dreamt, dreamed	träumen
drink	drank	drunk	trinken
drive	drove	driven	fahren
eat	ate	eaten	essen
fall	fell	fallen	fallen
feel	felt	felt	fühlen
fight	fought	fought	kämpfen
find	found	found	finden
forbid	forbade	forbidden	verbieten, untersagen
forecast	forecast, forecasted	forecast, forecasted	vorhersagen
forget	forgot	forgotten	vergessen
forgive	forgave	forgiven	vergeben, verzeihen
freeze	froze	frozen	einfrieren, gefrieren
get	got	got	bekommen
give	gave	given	geben
go	went	gone	gehen
grow	grew	grown	wachsen
hang	hung	hung	hängen
have	had	had	haben
hear	heard	heard	hören
hide	hid	hidden	verstecken
hit	hit	hit	schlagen, hauen
hold	held	held	halten
hurt	hurt	hurt	verletzen
keep	kept	kept	(be)halten, bewahren
kneel	knelt, kneeled	knelt, kneeled	knien
know	knew	known	kennen, wissen
lay	laid	laid	legen
lead	led	led	führen, leiten
lean	leant, leaned	leant, leaned	lehnen
learn	learnt, learned	learnt, learned	lernen
leave	left	left	verlassen

Infinitive	Simple Past	Past Participle	German
lend	lent	lent	(ver)leihen
let	let	let	lassen
lie	lay	lain	liegen
lose	lost	lost	verlieren
make	made	made	machen, herstellen
mean	meant	meant	meinen, bedeuten
meet	met	met	treffen, begegnen
pay	paid	paid	bezahlen
put	put	put	setzen, stellen, legen
quit	quit, quitted	quit, quitted	beenden, verlassen
read	read	read	lesen
ride	rode	ridden	reiten, fahren (Rad)
rise	rose	risen	(an)steigen, aufgehen
run	ran	run	laufen
say	said	said	sagen
see	saw	seen	sehen
seek	sought	sought	suchen
sell	sold	sold	verkaufen
send	sent	sent	senden, verschicken
shake	shook	shaken	schütteln
show	showed	shown, showed	zeigen
shrink	shrank, shrunk	shrunk	schrumpfen, einlaufen
shut	shut	shut	schließen
sing	sang	sung	singen
sink	sank	sunk	sinken
sit	sat	sat	sitzen
sleep	slept	slept	schlafen
slide	slid	slid	rutschen, gleiten
smell	smelt, smelled	smelt, smelled	riechen
sow	sowed	sown, sowed	säen
speak	spoke	spoken	sprechen
speed	sped, speeded	sped, speeded	rasen, schnell fahren
spend	spent	spent	verbringen, ausgeben
spill	spilt, spilled	spilt, spilled	verschütten
split	split	split	teilen, spalten
stand	stood	stood	stehen
steal	stole	stolen	stehlen
stick	stuck	stuck	kleben, haften
sting	stung	stung	stechen
sweat	sweat, sweated	sweat, sweated	schwitzen
sweep	swept	swept	fegen, kehren
swing	swung	swung	schwingen, schwenken
take	took	taken	nehmen
teach	taught	taught	lehren, unterrichten
tear	tore	torn	zerreißen
tell	told	told	erzählen
think	thought	thought	denken, glauben
throw	threw	thrown	werfen
understand	understood	understood	verstehen
wake	woke, waked	woken, waked	(auf)wecken, aufwachen
wear	wore	worn	tragen (Kleidung)
win	won	won	gewinnen
wind	wound	wound	winden, aufziehen (Uhr)
write	wrote	written	schreiben

A1PIX - Your Photo Today, Taufkirchen: 68.2 (Rolf Zscharnack); adpic Bildagentur, Bonn: 2.3 (C. Schwier); alamy images, Abingdon/Oxfordshire: 12.3, 68.5, 68.6; Berghahn, Matthias, Illustrator, Bielefeld: 21.1, 21.2, 21.3, 22.1, 41.1, 87.1, 93.1; bildagentur-online GmbH, Burgkunstadt: 36.2 (Begsteiger); Caro Fotoagentur GmbH, Berlin: 65.3 (Hoffmann); Corbis, Düsseldorf: 12.1 (Helen King); dreamstime.com, Brentwood: 2.1; Druwe & Polastri, Cremlingen/Weddel: 36.1; EK AUTOMATION GmbH, Rosengarten/Nenndorf: 92.2; Europen, Brussels: 70.1 (Patrick Mascart); fml-Lehrstuhl für Fördertechnik Materialfluss Logistik TU München, Garching bei München: 61.2; Fotex Medien Agentur GmbH, Hamburg: 63.1 (Christoph Schweitzer); fotolia.com, New York: 2.5 (Hellen Sergeyeva), 12.2 (wildworx), 65.2 (Nimbus), 65.4 (Kirsty Pargeter), 68.4 (Mikhail Basov); getty images Deutschland GmbH, München: 2.2 (visuals unlimited); IPON, Berlin: 63.3 (Stefan Boness); Jungheinrich AG, Hamburg: 92.1, 92.4, 92.5, 92.6, 92.5, 92.6; KBS Industrieelektronik GmbH, Freiburg: 61.1, 61.3; Keystone Pressedienst, Hamburg: 61.4 (Ecken, Dominique); Picture-Alliance GmbH, Frankfurt/Main: 36.4, 63.4; ratioform Verpackungen GmbH, Pliening: 2.4; STILL GmbH, Hamburg: 92.3, 92.7, 92.8; Stills-Online Bildagentur, Hamburg: 65.1, 65.6, 68.1, 68.3; vario images, Bonn: 36.3; Vielhauer, Stefanie, Gelsenkirchen: 65.5; Visum Foto GmbH, Hamburg: 36.5, 63.2 (Holde Schneider), 63.5 (Achenbach & Pacini).

Alle Grafiken: Daniela Ringhut, Dreieich.

Die in diesem Produkt gemachten Angaben zu Unternehmen (Namen, Internet- und E-Mail-Adressen, Handelsregistereintragungen, Bankverbindungen, Steuer-, Telefon- und Faxnummern und alle weiteren Angaben) sind i.d.R. fiktiv, d.h., sie stehen in keinem Zusammenhang mit einem real existierenden Unternehmen in der dargestellten oder einer ähnlichen Form. Dies gilt auch für alle Kunden, Lieferanten und sonstigen Geschäftspartner der Unternehmen wie z.B. Kreditinstitute, Versicherungsunternehmen und andere Dienstleistungsunternehmen. Ausschließlich zum Zwecke der Authentizität werden die Namen real existierender Unternehmen und z.B. im Fall von Kreditinstituten auch deren IBANs und BICs verwendet.

Die in diesem Werk aufgeführten Internetadressen sind auf dem Stand zum Zeitpunkt der Drucklegung. Die ständige Aktualität der Adressen kann vonseiten des Verlages nicht gewährleistet werden. Darüber hinaus übernimmt der Verlag keine Verantwortung für die Inhalte dieser Seiten.